Pocket Change

Pocket Change:

Using the Science of Personal Change
To Improve Financial Habits

Heidi T. Beckman

EP Effertrux Publishing
Sun Prairie, Wisconsin

Effertrux Publishing
P.O. Box 694
Sun Prairie, WI 53590-9998
United States of America
www.Effertrux.com

The author has been careful to confirm the accuracy of the information presented in this book and to ensure that it is based on research results that are considered to be sound and acceptable to the scientific community at the time of publication of this work (that is, the research results have been published in peer-reviewed journals). However, the author is not responsible for errors or omissions or for any consequences resulting from the application of the ideas in this book. The author does not guarantee that any particular outcome will occur in the lives of the readers of this book. The information in this work is not intended as a substitute for consultation with financial professionals. The examples and stories that are relayed in this book are composites of true stories; the names and identifying details of the people involved have been changed to protect the anonymity of these individuals.

Editing by Daniel Meinen

ISBN: 978-0985842789

Library of Congress Control Number: 2013943200

Reviewers

To Mom, Dad, Dawn, and Dan

Table of Contents

Section IV

Section I

Chapter One:
Understanding the Problem

"The biggest room in the world is the room for improvement."

-Japanese Proverb

"Winning at money is 80 percent behavior and 20 percent head knowledge...Most of us know what to do, but we just don't do it."

-Dave Ramsey

"For every complex problem there is an easy answer, and it is wrong."

-H. L. Mencken

"What are you doing in there?" my mother called down the hallway. She knew, as all good mothers do, that when the house grew strangely quiet, her three-year-old daughter was up to some kind of mischief. Thankfully, the mischief I preferred was relatively harmless. I could spend hours emptying the contents of my mother's purse onto the pale yellow bedroom carpet and then replacing them again.

Part of the attraction may have been the opportunity to practice newly-acquired motor skills by opening and closing zippers, snaps, and ties. Still, there was something more to my fascination with handbags. I am certain that my toddler brain was lured by a sense of abundance. To think that this elegant, powder blue leather clutch was so compact, and yet it hid a world of treasures deep within its fabric lining. From keys to breath mints to a wallet and its rich contents, it was all there, it was accessible at any moment, and you could be the owner of it all simply by grasping the frayed, brown leather handle.

Eventually, my mother placed a substitute purse with unbreakable contents within my reach for me to find while she hid her "real" purse on a closet shelf. I guess she did not want her library card eaten and her lipstick used as a crayon. Imagine her delight when she eventually found and purchased a children's book called "What's in Mommy's Pocketbook?"[1] The book was interactive and allowed kids to remove paper objects from the pockets within the story's pages and place them in a tiny pocketbook. Then, the story prompted children to put all of the objects back in their proper hiding places.

There were the paper spectacles, which were bold, classic mod frames from the 1960's. Then there was the diamond ring, which, if it were the genuine article rather than paper, would have been about twenty carat. Most importantly, there were the shiny, silver coins. The coins were pocket change that represented a sense of wealth, ownership, and power in a world where three-year-olds feel small. You could touch them, manipulate them, and move them in or out of the pocketbook. You could pretend to save them or pretend to spend them. It was the very beginning of my journey to understand the impact of human behavior upon money.

Later in life, I decided to study this formally, as I completed a degree in clinical psychology and also became a Certified Educator in Personal Finance. At present, I work in the field of health psychology, a specialty area that focuses on understanding how psychological and social factors influence health habits which, in turn, impact our coping and well-being.

Working with patients who have a variety of health conditions, I have met hundreds of individuals who needed to make changes in personal health habits or lifestyle in order to optimize their ability to cope with illness. For example, I've met patients with diabetes who needed to eat healthier, exercise more, or be more consistent about checking their blood sugar levels. I've met patients with neurological conditions who needed to reduce anxiety and tension, and chronic pain patients who needed to modify the negative thoughts and emotions that contribute to pain flare-ups.

The task that each patient faces is personal change, and *personal change is notoriously difficult*. That's why 45% of people give up on their New Year's resolutions before the end of January, and 88% of all resolutions end in failure.[2] It's also why so many members of our society struggle with obesity, and a multi-billion dollar diet industry has evolved. In the field of medicine, it's why so many people are addicted to the wrong stuff (nicotine, narcotics), and so many people fail to take the right stuff (multivitamins, leafy greens, medications for high blood pressure).

Problems with personal change plague us in the financial realm, as well. The failure of Americans to make positive changes to their money habits led to a significant rise in the level of consumer debt for many years, until the trend was finally tempered by the recent economic crisis.

Most experts would agree that at this point, our nation is still in trouble. Studies have shown that about 43 percent of American families spend more than they earn each year. According to recent reports, many Americans have little to no savings as retirement approaches, forcing them to consider working well into their 60's and 70's. According to a survey by the Employee Benefit Research Institute, more than half of all workers (56%) say they have less than $25,000 in retirement savings and investments[3]—a situation that does not bode well for their financial futures.

The challenge of modifying health habits and the challenge of transforming money habits are similar. Both endeavors call to mind concepts such as willpower, persistence, strength, and fortitude. Each year in the United States, millions of individuals resolve themselves to lose weight, exercise more, eliminate debt, reduce spending, or make better contributions to their retirement plans. Then, each year, millions of individuals are disappointed when their change efforts fall short.

Let's take a look at two examples:

A Tale of Two Changers

Sam, age 57, had been smoking cigarettes since he was 12 years old. He knew about the health consequences of nicotine usage. His doctor gave him "the lecture" numerous times. Each time the doctor lectured, Sam thought to himself, "My Grandpa Charlie smoked his whole life and lived to the ripe old age of 97. We're just not affected by nicotine in our family the way the rest of the world is."

There was one incident that gave Sam pause for thought. His seven-year-old granddaughter was visiting after school one day. She had learned in class that day about the dangers of smoking cigarettes. She pleaded with him to quit, and the message got through. Two days later, Sam decided to throw away all of his packs of cigarettes except one, which he hid between two pairs of grey crew socks in a dresser drawer just in case of an "emergency."

He did well for a while. He did not give in to the cravings despite the discomfort of withdrawal. He remembered his granddaughter's distress and felt confident that he could remain smoke-free. His success lasted about six weeks.

Then, one day at work, he needed to find a particular coworker who happened to be outside in the designated smoking area. When offered a cigarette, Sam accepted after only a slight hesitation. He felt that he had been working hard and he deserved something that would "take the edge off." He fully intended to enjoy just one cigarette, no more. From then on, the smoking habit returned in full force.

Cathy has been overutilizing credit for a number of years now. She acquired her first credit card in college. She was hungry and running off to class, and there was a representative standing on the commons offering free pizza to anyone who filled out a credit card application. When she received the card, she used it responsibly enough that she qualified for more credit cards, and then even more. By the time she completed graduate school and got settled in her first job, she had multiple bank and store credit cards.

Unfortunately, the debt piled up. Cathy was aware that if she lost her job, there was not enough money in her savings to keep paying the credit card bills. She was also aware that after paying bills each month, she had no money left over to save for her retirement. Cathy preferred not to think about the risks. Each time her financial planner lectured to her, she thought, "I'm not a sucker. In fact, I'm pretty resourceful. I've got a degree and intelligence and creativity that other people don't have. I wouldn't be affected by a financial downturn the way the rest of the world is."

There was one incident that prompted temporary change. She got word that the company she worked for was downsizing. No one was quite sure who would lose their jobs. Suddenly, her credit card balances weighed heavily on her mind. In a moment of clarity, she grabbed a pair of scissors and cut up all of her credit cards except one. She scribbled "For Emergencies Only!" on a yellow post-it note, stuck it on the credit card that was spared, and tucked the card away at the back of her wallet.

Although she missed her frequent shopping trips at first, she now had extra time that she could use to connect with her family or strengthen her dedication to work projects. Distraction seemed to work well for her. That is, it worked well until she started feeling left out of the shopping trips planned by her coworkers.

Sensing her despondence but not understanding her financial situation, her coworkers invited her to join them on their next retail adventure. Cathy agreed to go, promising herself that she would just browse and would not buy anything. When she set foot in her favorite store, she was blinded by the best and the brightest of the spring fashion line, and she could not even see that she was hovering precariously over the edge of the slippery slope.

The Problem

Sam and Cathy both knew, deep down inside, that change was warranted in their lives. But they preferred to keep that reality tucked neatly away most of the time. There was an occasional jolt that dislodged frightening thoughts now and then. Sometimes the fears even mobilized personal change efforts. However, the old habits eventually returned.

One of the most interesting things about Sam and Cathy is that neither of them suffered from a knowledge or information deficit. Neither of them could honestly say they *didn't know* that their behavior could hurt them in the long run, or that they didn't know there were resources available to help them change for the better. Sam and Cathy had multiple people in their lives who tried to give them information about the problem.

Sam's primary care physician had given him a variety of pamphlets and brochures about smoking cessation products, local quit-assist programs, and the health hazards of tobacco. Cathy's husband had given her a book about personal finance. One of her coworkers said great things about a particular credit counseling agency that she recommended. Cathy's financial planner gave her lists of books, websites, and financial planning tools to help her improve her situation. For both Sam and Cathy, the tools and resources were plentiful, but information was simply not enough to correct the problem.

This brings us to the starting point of the book. For most people who are stuck in the process of personal change, the problem is NOT an information deficit. *The problem is a gap between intention and action.* This fits with what I have observed in my role as a psychologist. By the time clients reach my office, chances are good that they have already met with multiple intelligent, supportive, well-meaning professionals who have tried to facilitate behavior change by providing them with information. The information, however, does not generate or enhance motivation. During my first meeting with clients, the phrase I hear most often is "I know what I need to do; I just can't make myself do it." The task, then, is to find new and creative ways to move forward.

The truth is that having knowledge of a problem does not guarantee that you can make the problem go away. Human behavior is complex and determined by multiple factors. The part of the brain that is responsible for self-control and self-restraint, the prefrontal cortex, has developed and expanded during human evolution, but it is still easily overtaxed. Research in neuroscience shows that when you experience the stress of multiple demands, the prefrontal cortex is not strong enough to manage this cognitive load, and you lose the ability to use good judgment. At the same time, your emotions interact with and influence your attention, memory, and reasoning. This means that emotional factors figure into the motivation equation, as well.

The good news is that scientists are discovering important clues that will help you enhance your motivation for change. For example, there is evidence that certain types of distraction can effectively help people delay gratification when they feel like giving in to a temptation.[4] There is also evidence that individuals who practice mental discipline in one area strengthen their ability to use self-restraint in other areas.[5]

The bad news is that many of the people in our society who are in a position to help others change (the "front line" helpers such as educators, credit counselors, and financial planners) still use advice-giving as their primary mode of intervention. Advice-giving often creates psychological resistance on the part of the recipient. Advisees sense that their autonomy is being threatened on some level, and so they dig in their heels to prevent the loss of freedom, like the freedom to buy expensive coffee drinks or to spend their whole paycheck on "wants" instead of "needs."

The formal name for this idea is reactance theory, which was originally proposed by Jack Brehm[6] and later was extended to clinical psychology by Sharon Brehm.[7] According to this theory, individuals may nod their heads in agreement with the advice that is being dispensed to them, but deep inside, there is a little voice that is yelling, "No way! I am not going to be the only person who saves 15% of my paycheck when all of my coworkers are driving fancy new cars."

The biggest problem with advice-giving, then, is that it generates resistance. Another problem is that it places the recipient of advice in a passive role, like a sponge that is supposed to soak up wisdom. Unfortunately, this does a disservice to the advisee because to succeed with behavior change, people need to be active, observant, dynamic, and flexible. We are generally not motivated to work toward goals that others have set for us based on their agendas. We need to be able to take ownership of a goal, to interact with the goal, and to become active problem solvers in order to figure out how to reach it.

In the money domain, it is easy to see why so many financial advisers assume the role of educators and advice-givers. It is certainly true that there is a lack of formalized, systematic financial education in this country. In many school districts, it is possible to get through elementary and secondary education without learning a thing about the essentials of personal finance or basic economics.

However, that's not the main problem. When you are obese, you do not need to know the intricacies of satiety mechanisms, metabolic processes, or exercise physiology in order to manage weight. You simply need to know that to lose weight, "calories out" must exceed "calories in."

In the same way, when you are struggling with finances, you do not need to know how the market in China affects the economy of the United States, nor do you need to know how to evaluate the quarterly performance of mutual funds. You simply need to know that to improve your financial standing, "money in" must exceed "money out." Most people possess this basic knowledge, whether they were formally educated about it or not. They get stuck when they intend to apply this truth to their own lives and find out how challenging it is to be consistently motivated.

To be clear, it is not just individuals who are struggling with financial survival whose knowledge of proper financial habits fails to be translated into authentic action. There are people at all socioeconomic levels, in all occupations, and in all walks of life who find that they cannot execute their best laid financial plans.

Research in the area of human information processing and cognitive biases documents how frequently people make seemingly irrational or illogical decisions when it comes to money.[8] Like my clients who lament, "I know what I need to do; I just can't bring myself to do it," many intelligent people across this country repeat a similar refrain in the offices of their financial advisers.

In response, multiple "voices of reason" attempt to dispense advice and information. You hear sound bites from significant others, parents, coworkers, bankers, business partners, and television news anchors. You get advice from creatively titled self-help books, like *You Should Just Listen to Me, and You Will Become Wealthy* (OK, it's not an actual book title, but it's close enough).

Take a step back and evaluate this approach. When you get advice from experts or professionals, do you grab the knowledge that they impart and run with it? Or does that little voice of reactance theory speak up inside your head, asking "If I take this advice, won't I be giving up some of my freedom to do what I want with my money in the future?" If you *do* decide to listen to the advice of others, how motivated are you to work toward goals that were derived from their agendas, not your own? Are you able to make the transition from passive recipient of information to active crusader for financial change? Most of the time, the answer is "no."

If it is not reactance theory getting in your way, then there are many other ways to sabotage yourself. You can fool yourself into thinking that there is something wrong with your external circumstances--if you just find the right financial adviser or the right job, all of the money will fall into place. Of course, much of the time it is your *internal* landscape that needs the most attention. As the classic adage promises, "Wherever you go, there you are." If you do not adjust your internal environment, you carry your flawed financial habits into each new set of life conditions.

Let's examine some of the other ways that people fool themselves about the concept of personal change.

Myths About Personal Change

- *Change is linear.* It is much easier to entertain the notion of change if you picture a map, consider yourself to be at point "A," consider your end goal to be at point "B," and map out the journey as the crow flies. Ideally, the path toward a goal would be a straight line. In reality, though, change is more of a winding road where you stop by the road and rest for a while, or even take a wrong turn or two. Tal Ben-Shahar, psychology professor at Harvard University, describes the path toward a goal as an "irregular upward spiral...[with] numerous deviations along the way."[9] The key point is that change takes practice, patience, and a repeated "coming back" to your goal.

- *Change is all-or-nothing.* It is tempting to think about change as absolute: either you make it to a goal, or you don't; either you achieve an outcome, or you fail. In reality, change is complex, and you often find yourself in the grey area between the black and white extremes. Ultimately, if you can increase your tolerance for ambiguity and accept the fact that failure and achievement are inextricably linked, you will persist and grow.[10]

- *Change should happen in one try.* Actually, change is so difficult, the average self-changer has to make several attempts before succeeding. Researchers Prochaska, Norcross, and DiClemente first discovered this when studying the change efforts of individuals who were addicted to substances such as alcohol, drugs, or cigarettes. They learned that most people who quit smoking report three or four serious attempts before they finally manage to kick the habit. Later, they extended their research to other types of personal change and found similar results. For instance, they found that people typically have to make a resolution for five consecutive years or more before it becomes a permanent change.[11]

One reason that change is so difficult is because our minds are divided into independent systems that sometimes conflict. Psychologist Jonathan Haidt uses the analogy of the Elephant (the emotional side of the brain) and the Rider (the rational side of the brain).[12] The emotional side feels pain and pleasure and likes instant gratification. The rational side is analytical and strategic and can mull over decisions with great aplomb. When I receive my paycheck and make careful plans to spend it in the most responsible way possible, I am exercising the specialty skills of the Rider. When I blow my paycheck at the electronics store, I am allowing the Elephant to have his way.

The Rider sits on top of the Elephant, holds the reins, and appears to be in charge most of the time. However, because he is small, he will lose to the Elephant whenever they conflict. For change to happen, there must be a goal that appeals to both the Elephant and the Rider. This does not always happen on the first attempt at change.

- *Once you achieve initial success, it is all downhill from there.* Although it is quite nice to experience the initial taste of pride, satisfaction, and reward when you succeed at taking the first few steps toward your goal, the remainder of the journey just gets more difficult. In fact, it is almost guaranteed that the next set of emotions you will experience includes frustration, hardship, self-doubt, and even hopelessness. It is quite easy to get defeated when you are trying to persist at a change effort and it feels like a struggle. Thankfully, research on the "growth mindset"[13] has shown us an alternative to defeatism. People who know from the beginning that "everything is hard before it is easy" and who recognize struggles as learning opportunities are able to persist and to succeed in the end.

- *Change is just a matter of willpower.* When change researchers Prochaska, Norcross, and DiClemente interviewed successful changers and asked them how they made change happen, the universal response was "willpower." However, when they asked these individuals to define willpower, they got a wide array of answers and respondents described almost every imaginable change technique.[14]

If willpower refers to every conceivable method of change, then it is inevitable that it takes willpower to change. However, if willpower is used in a narrower sense, meaning "a belief in our abilities to change behavior, and the decision to act on that belief,"[14] then it is important to remember that this is only one of several possible strategies available to you. There are many possible routes to successful change.

The Solution

As it turns out, despite the difficulty of personal change, people can and do change successfully. You are not destined to be the passive recipient of advice that may or may not fit your unique situation. A wealth of theory and research on the subject of behavior change is available in the psychology journals, and you can apply it easily to your money habits. I will refer to these strategies, gathered from the science of personal change, as the new behavior change technologies. Several of these principles and theories will be featured in this book.

In my role as a psychologist, I help clients apply these technologies to improve their habits and optimize their ability to cope with stress and illness. It is gratifying to watch clients become "unstuck" and to witness remarkable transformations that support improved physical and emotional health.

The same change technologies can be applied in the domain of personal finance. The ideas have the power to transform the way that you think and behave in relation to money, and the power to improve your bottom line. In this book, I will introduce you to these ideas and assist you as you apply them to your financial situation. In the process, you will learn how to close the gulf between intention and action when it comes to your money habits. You will also learn how to create the motivation, the framework, and the lifestyle elements that support financial health.

Organization of the Book

It always helps to begin a change effort with the proper mindset, and chapter two will help you to shape this mindset as you prepare for the twists and turns of the change process. Chapter three will help you craft a financial goal that will guide you as you apply the material in the remainder of the book. It will also help you pinpoint the specific situations in which it will be crucial to practice your new habits. After designing a goal, you need to choose a method for tracking your progress over time (a concept known as self-monitoring). Chapter four will summarize the research on self-monitoring and help you select an appropriate tracking system.

Section two of the book provides the "meat" of some of the major psychological theories of change and helps you apply them to your money goals. Chapter five introduces the *transtheoretical model* and its construct of the *stages of change*. This is a model that will help you determine your state of readiness for change. Once you determine your initial starting point, you will have important clues about what you need to do to move ahead from one stage to another. Chapter six describes the concept of *self-efficacy*, which is your belief in your ability to organize and carry out the courses of action necessary to achieve your goal. This personal belief influences the choices you make, the effort you put forth in working toward your goal, how long you persist when confronted with obstacles, and how you feel in the process of working toward goals.

Chapter seven explores the concept of *persistence*, or what it takes to maintain consistent action in pursuit of a goal. Various lines of research suggest how to support tenacity. Many of these suggestions may help you maintain your change efforts over time. But persistence cannot stand alone; it must be accompanied by *impulse control* to help you withstand the temptations that threaten to take you off of your path. In chapter eight, you will learn that impulse control is an exhaustible resource. You will learn what actions you can take to sustain your goal-directed efforts despite a diminishing supply of self-control.

Of course, change does not occur in a vacuum. It occurs in the context of your beliefs, experiences, and interactions with the world. If you make individual change efforts without taking the larger context into consideration, your efforts may get stymied. In section three, you will learn how to align your environment (chapter nine), social relationships (chapter ten), thoughts (chapter eleven), and emotions (chapter twelve) with your change goals. This will help tip the scales of habit modification in your favor.

The final section of the book, section four, helps you design a plan for avoiding or dealing with future money-related problems. Chapter thirteen helps you distinguish between an initial setback or lapse and a larger relapse. It offers methods for troubleshooting when you feel stuck and disappointed with your change efforts. Chapter fourteen offers ideas for maintaining your new desired habits over time. It helps you design an individualized relapse prevention plan. It also helps you examine the overall place of money in your life.

I have a special request for how you use this book. Rather than reading through it in one sitting, consider absorbing small bits of material and then taking the time to be thoughtful and reflective as you apply them to your own situation. To help slow down the pace of reading, I have provided reflection questions and activities at the end of each chapter. These exercises will help you develop a more potent and nuanced understanding of the complex issue of personal change.

Change is certainly not a one-size-fits-all endeavor, and it will take mental work on your end to tailor the material to your unique circumstances. You have nothing to lose by taking your time and processing the issues deeply, and you might even learn something interesting about yourself. Dig deep and enjoy it!

Reflection Questions

How do you react when people you know (family members, friends, coworkers, financial advisers) give you financial advice? Have you ever heard the voice of reactance theory in your head, and what did it say? Are you more likely to make changes when people give you advice, or when you feel internally motivated to make something better in your life?

Have you ever fallen prey to the idea that if only something changed in your external circumstances, the money would fall into place? For example, "If only I got that advancement at work, then I would not have financial struggles." If you truly, honestly examine this line of thinking, do you believe that it is accurate? If not, where is the flaw in this reasoning? What really needs to change in your life?

Think about the personal changes you have made successfully in your life, and try to recall the details about the *process* of change that you went through. Did change occur as an immediate transformation? Or did it take practice, trial and error, and a repeated "coming back" to your goal?

It can be daunting to work on the first of fourteen chapters about personal change. Take a moment, look at the big picture, and give yourself credit for all that you have accomplished already. Think about all of the efforts you have made, either large or small, to improve the health of your finances. Every effort counts, whether it got you results or not. Think about all of the articles and books you've read, all of the people you've consulted, and all of the gold stars you've already earned for your efforts. And give yourself two more gold stars: one for getting this book, and another for finishing chapter one!

<u>Activities</u>

Spend some time with your financial dreams! Make a list of ten of your dreams. Consider what you would like to have in life, but also consider what you would like to be, do, and give. Some of your dreams may be practical (getting out of debt; sending the kids to college), while others may be more extravagant (purchasing your dream home; traveling to French Polynesia once each year during your retirement; funding a scholarship at your college alma mater).

For each dream that you listed, ask yourself the following question: "On a scale of 0-10, where "0" is no motivation at all to make this dream happen, and "10" is an abundant, overflowing sense of passion, desire, and motivation to make this dream happen, what rating do I give?" Write your rating next to each goal.

Now review your list of dreams and the corresponding ratings. Where is the potential for forward movement? Which dreams would be *worth* the investment of energy required to make them come true? Narrow down your list to your top three dreams. This will help you choose an area of focus as you move on to the next chapters.

Chapter Two:
Preparing for Change

"If I had six hours to chop down a tree, I'd spend the first hour sharpening the ax."

-Abraham Lincoln

"If you want to increase your success rate, double your failure rate."

-Thomas T. Watson

I have had the good fortune of attending a couple of recent conferences on "peak performance," also known as elite or optimal performance. Many of the leaders in this field are sports psychologists who work with professional athletes who want to stay at the top of their game. When you see an incredible sports performance on the world stage, chances are good that there was a sports psychologist working behind the scenes.

Of course, for every sporting event, there is a threshold of physiological performance that cannot be surpassed. There is an ultimate limit to what the human body can achieve. If there were not such a limit, then we would eventually see high jumpers able to clear the Empire State Building or runners able to complete a one-minute mile.

Trainers in the sports world have learned that when the resources of the body are optimized, the brain becomes the tool that gives athletes a competitive edge. The brain has become the new frontier to be explored in order to facilitate peak performance. If an athlete can learn to improve his focus and self-regulation skills, he may gain the advantage that will allow him to outperform others who have undergone a similar level of physical training.

The competitive edge and the elite status come from purposeful work called "deliberate practice."[1] Individuals who pursue deliberate practice do not just engage in the mechanical repetition of a task. They break the task down into its requisite skills, assess their performance on these skills, and then design subgoals that allow them to adjust their execution of the task over and over again until they get closer to the desired outcome.

And so it is with habit change. Let's take the goal of healthy eating as an example. When it comes to the goal of healthy eating, you might consider the members of the National Weight Control Registry[2] to be the elite performers. The National Weight Control Registry is a system that tracks and researches individuals who have been successful with long-term weight loss maintenance. In order to qualify for the registry, an individual must have maintained at least a 30-pound weight loss for one year or longer. There are currently over 5,000 individuals listed in the registry.

If you ask these individuals how they attained success, they will tell you they did not just decide to "eat healthy" and then mindlessly repeat the same food routine every day. Instead, they took stock of what they did well and what they did not do well. They decided what habits to throw away entirely (like the Friday evening tradition of going to the pizza buffet), what habits to keep (a piece of fruit as a morning snack), and what habits to tweak. They designed specific subgoals, practiced their execution, and continually adjusted their habits over and over again until they made progress toward the overall goals of weight loss and maintenance.

Deliberate practice is just as important in the world of personal finance as it is in the realm of sports or health. Individuals who successfully change a financial habit for the long term typically do not make this change overnight. First they break through all of the denial and excuses that have built up over the years and identify their specific deficits. Then, they choose which new task to tackle. They break the task down into the requisite skills and design a plan for practice. Successful changers approach practice with an attitude of *experimentation*—if an experiment doesn't work, it gives them important data about what they can tweak on the next iteration of the task.

This strategy works. It's laboratory-tested and research-approved. However, most people simply don't use this approach to modify their money habits. Consider, for example, one of the most popular New Year's resolutions that makes it into the "top five" lists every year: "Save more money." If Americans were successfully meeting that resolution, they would not have to declare it every year. We would not be in our current financial dilemma with millions of people spending more money than they earn and a generation of workers approaching retirement with little to no savings.

We are failing to meet this resolution because instead of the deliberate practice strategy, Americans are using what I call the *January 1st strategy*: Set a vague, non-measurable, non-specific goal for yourself at the coldest, darkest, most stressful time of year; make sure you don't have adequate time to prepare for change (because, after all, you were busy with the holidays); make unsystematic efforts to approach that goal; and then put yourself down each time you fail—thereby decreasing your energy, focus, and motivation, as well as your chances that you will ever make that resolution again.

When you *do* succeed at reaching a personal finance goal, success doesn't happen dramatically, spontaneously, or because the calendar tells you that it happens to be January. Instead, successful change efforts follow a long period of gestation and preparation. Special "mental work" occurs before you reach the stage of goal-implementation (see chapter five for full treatment of this topic). When you are ready to exercise your new habits, you follow a detailed plan that you have carefully crafted in advance. You have a methodical way of dealing with setbacks, making sure they do not send you spiraling into thoughts of self-disappointment and defeat.

How do you achieve the attitude of experimentation, the patience for deliberate practice, and the immunity from feelings of hopelessness and despair? To begin a change effort with the proper mindset, you must first be willing to part with a few popular beliefs:

- *"I am waiting for the economy to improve (or my paycheck to increase, or my financial adviser to find the right investment, and so forth...)."* Most of the time, if you find yourself sitting and waiting, you can be fairly certain that you have slipped into a passive coping stance. Individuals who employ *passive* coping withdraw from the very activities that would help them move forward, and they depend upon outside circumstances to bring them relief. In contrast, individuals who employ *active* coping assume responsibility for their own self-management no matter how challenging the situation becomes. Research has found passive coping to be predictive of increased depression and stress. Active coping is related to *lower* levels of distress and helplessness. Active coping, then, strengthens the change mindset.

- *"I can't make myself do things that I don't really want to do."* If that were true, then you would never complete a single unpleasant task. It turns out that you don't necessarily have to *want* to do something in order to be *willing* to do it. When you are willing to do something, you accept the task because it supports one of your higher values. I don't really want to balance my checkbook every weekend, but I am willing to because I value self-awareness, security, and planning. You may not want to learn the total cost of all of your debt, but you are willing to because you value your future financial freedom and peace of mind.

- *"I will wait until I am inspired."* Both research and life experience teach us that if we wait for inspiration to descend upon us, we might be waiting a long time. However, if we change our behavior first, then inspiration and motivation will follow. This wisdom dates all the way back to Aristotle who explained that we become disciplined by first exercising good self-control, and we become courageous by first performing acts of courage. This technique has multiple names ("acting as-if," the "do good, be good approach," and "fake it 'til you make it") and lots of scientific support.

Consider what this means for your money habits. If you have $100 deducted from your monthly paycheck and automatically deposited into your savings account, you watch the savings begin to grow. Then, you are able to cultivate a sense of yourself as a "saver" or as a disciplined steward of your money. This leads you to make other decisions that are consistent with your new interpretation of yourself.

- *"I can make a solid effort at habit change for a while and then relax a bit."* The road to success often requires self-discipline, or choosing long-term gain over short-term pleasure: resisting a cupcake in the service of losing weight, enduring the hardship of homework in order to achieve good grades, spending hours in training in order to win an athletic championship, or passing up the unplanned purchases to stick to the household budget.

Research has shown that self-discipline is a crucial factor in predicting people's future success. It forecasts who will be able to do what is required of them well into the future (and therefore achieve important goals) versus who will wander down the path of temptation. Instead of being thrown off course by disappointment, failure, adversity, boredom, or plateaus in progress, disciplined people will keep working strenuously toward goals over time. Instead of relaxing their efforts, they will keep forging ahead (think deliberate practice).

Before you excuse yourself from this discussion by declaring "I am not a disciplined person," keep in mind that discipline is not a fixed trait—something you are either born with or not. There is fascinating evidence that self-discipline can be taught and cultivated. Chapters seven and eight will address this matter in greater detail. For now, suffice it to say that habit change will require ongoing vigilance and a continual willingness to practice, but with the proper tools, this will not be as difficult as it sounds.

Now that you've given up these popular beliefs, let's take a look at strategies that will help you prepare for your change efforts with the proper mindset.

<u>Cultivate the Identity of a Changer</u>

If you can make your change efforts a larger part of your identity or self-concept, you will be more likely to make the kinds of decisions that support your end goal. At the same time, any change effort that violates your identity will be doomed to failure. This is supported by research on the "self-as-doer" construct developed by Linda Houser-Marko and Kennon Sheldon at the University of Missouri-Columbia.[3]

Houser-Marko and Sheldon demonstrated that the more you identify with a particular role, the more likely it is that you will participate in related behavior. More specifically, if you identify yourself as the "doer" of a particular behavior, you will behave in concordance with that identity even when obstacles or barriers arise in your path. For example, if you have a strong self-concept as a "runner," you will still put your running shoes on and go outside for a 5K even when storm clouds are gathering on the horizon.

In the realm of personal finance, if you identify strongly with the role of "saver," you will be able to keep your wallet firmly tucked away even when you are tempted by a doorbuster sale at your favorite store. If you identify with the role of "investor," you will pay attention to news about the market even when several other things compete for your attention.

Build your desired identity by completing the sentence stem: "I am _____." Examples include: "I am a budget-follower," "I am a debt-annihilator," or "I am a consistent saver." Then harness the power of identity by training yourself to think: *"I did it, and will continue to do it, because that's who I am."*[3]

Strengthen your self-concept by writing your identity statement on a set of post-it notes and sticking them in places where you see them throughout the day (bathroom mirror, refrigerator, steering wheel, computer monitor). Each time you see a note, read the statement slowly and attempt to absorb its meaning.

Challenge yourself to work your new identity statement into conversations. It will feel foreign and contrived at first, but it will become more meaningful as time passes. Houser-Marko and Sheldon suggest that you spend some time simply imagining yourself with unshaken motivation, no matter what the circumstances. Your repeated identification of yourself as the *doer* of an action will help you to sustain your goal-directed efforts for the long term.

<u>Make Your Intention to Change Public</u>

Be bold. Talk to other people (preferably supportive people) about your intention to change. There are many ways to enhance your sense of commitment to change, but one of the easiest and most effective ways is to make a public promise that you are working toward a goal. Tell your friends and family what you plan to do. Write it on a big sheet of paper and tape it to the refrigerator. Take out an ad in a local newspaper and tell the world about the challenge you are undertaking.

This works because it makes your change effort an issue of integrity in your own eyes and in the eyes of others.[4] We generally want to think of ourselves in a positive way, and we want others to think positively about us, as well. If we say publicly that we plan to accomplish something, we will go to great lengths to maintain our integrity; that is, to be consistent with our stated values and expectations.

Making a goal public also helps you to garner social support from important others and to create a positive emotional climate in which to achieve your dreams. Consider the science of social bonding and the brain. Scientists who study the brain have discovered that the limbic system, which functions as the brain's emotional center, is an open-loop system. This means that rather than being a closed system that does not exchange information with anyone outside of itself, the limbic system can transmit signals that alter the emotions and physiology of another person.[5] In addition, it regulates itself based on input from outside sources. The moral of the story is that emotions are "contagious" whenever people are near one another, even if the contact is nonverbal. It becomes important, then, for you to be around positive, inspiring people in order to generate a sense of possibility and to move ahead toward your goal. There is a direct path from a positive emotional climate to positive outcomes.

<u>Remember the Enthusiasm Curve</u>

How do you build your expectations for the change journey? It seems reasonable that you would want to set yourself up to feel optimistic and positive. But at the same time, you need to be realistic. If you just tell yourself that you will sail through the change process, then what will you do when change becomes difficult, as any worthwhile change effort does?

Chip and Dan Heath, in their book *Switch: How to Change Things When Change is Hard*, present a way to enter the change journey with reasonable expectations. They describe the "Project Mood Chart" developed by Tim Brown, the CEO at IDEO (which is one of the world's most successful product design firms). The project mood chart is "…a U-shaped curve with a peak of positive emotion, labeled 'hope,' at the beginning, and a second peak of emotion, labeled 'confidence,' at the end. In between the two peaks is a negative emotional valley labeled 'insight.'"[6]

Essentially, the team leaders at this company are trying to establish realistic expectations for the change journey. They are predicting that at the beginning of the project, energy and enthusiasm will flow easily. But soon after comes frustration, discouragement, doubt, and sometimes even helplessness or hopelessness. If team members remember that these feelings are a normal and natural part of the change journey, they can walk alongside the feelings, stay task-focused, and eventually develop the insight that will take them to a place of renewed confidence and personal efficacy.

In this model, falling down is not interpreted as "failure." *Falling down is interpreted as an expected and essential part of learning.* It is a sign that you are taking on a project that is challenging and worthwhile. And it can be used as a cue to remind yourself that you are building essential insights. This can help minimize feelings of hopelessness and discouragement.

In one of the health management groups I lead at my workplace, I once proposed to group members that when we slip up, instead of beating ourselves up in our heads, we should wish ourselves a cheerful "Good failure!" The group members loved it. We all know that we have to fall down a few times before we can learn to run, but we don't really have an expression in our language that reminds us of that fact.

The idea that slip-ups are normal and natural is ancient wisdom that is just now getting encoded into modern schools of psychotherapy. Looking at Eastern philosophy, you find that a basic principle of Buddhist thought is that our existence is characterized by suffering. Buddhists believe that our attitude toward suffering predicts how we will cope with it when it arises. If we have a strong desire to be free of suffering and actively try to push it away, we actually invite more suffering into our lives. However, if we adopt an attitude that allows greater tolerance of suffering, we place ourselves on the path to enlightenment or emotional freedom.

A modern school of psychotherapy, called acceptance and commitment therapy (ACT), is centered around this idea. In this school of thought, acceptance is not giving up, passively resigning, or taking a defeatist stance. It is an active, positive embracing of one's experience, including the emotional challenges. Individuals are taught that the more they try to avoid failure, the more they suffer, because their efforts at avoidance are based on restricting their life or themselves in some way. However, if they accept the setbacks that inevitably come along, they can commit to the life goals and endeavors that give them a sense of meaning and purpose, and they can live the full, vital life that they wish to live.

Taking all of this into account, if you were to give yourself a good pep talk at the outset of your financial change project, it might sound something like this: *"I am a power-saver! Now is the time that I can prove that I am worthy of that luxurious trip around the world that I will take during my retirement. When the world tempts me to spend money that I should be saving, I will shout, 'No, world, you can't trick me into that!' And when I falter, I will say to myself, 'Good failure, my friend! This just proves that I have taken on a goal that is worth my time, attention, and effort. And this proves that I am moving forward and making progress. I will embrace the doubts and discouragement and frustration and walk with them to the finish line!'"*

Adopt a Growth Mindset

Stanford University psychologist Carol Dweck has conducted decades of research about the power of *mindset* in influencing one's approach to goals.[7] The conclusions she has reached teach us important lessons about persistence.

Dweck found that some people approach their goals with a "fixed mindset." They believe that for any given ability, you either have it or you don't, and your abilities simply reflect the way you are wired. Your fundamental qualities (like intelligence, athleticism, money management, or business sense, for example) are perceived as static. Therefore, when an opportunity comes along to strengthen a particular ability, these individuals avoid the challenge, get defensive, or see their effort as fruitless. In the mind of individuals with a fixed mindset, setbacks simply confirm failure and prove that they lack ability. They see no point in attempting anything too hard, because they might just end up looking or feeling deficient in some way.

In contrast, some people approach their goals with a "growth mindset." They believe that abilities are like muscles that get strengthened with practice. When a challenge comes along, these individuals embrace the challenge, persist in the face of obstacles, and view effort as the path to mastery. They take risks, accept feedback, and take the long-term perspective. They know that setbacks do not mean failure or ultimate defeat. Instead, blunders mean an opportunity to learn from mistakes and to use the feedback or criticism to reach successively higher levels of achievement.

Obviously, it is much easier to persist toward a goal when every mistake does not signal eventual failure. But how do you adopt a growth mindset if this is not the mindset that comes naturally to you? Dweck offers broad suggestions and specific ideas to help with this task. The broad suggestions include the following:

- Remind yourself that everything is hard before it becomes easy.

- Remind yourself that everything can look like failure in the middle of a change endeavor.

- If you see something that looks like failure, remember that it is simply a sign that you are making progress and that you have taken on a worthwhile project or goal.

- Remember that your commitment is to growth, and you can always find lessons and inspiration in your life experiences.

The specific ideas come from Dweck's growth mindset workshop which she describes in her book.[7] She stresses the importance of getting specific about the "when, where, and how" in reference to something that you want to learn or a problem that you need to confront.

For instance, she proposes that every morning as you think about the day ahead of you, ask yourself: "What are the opportunities for learning and growth today? For myself? For the people around me?" Then, as you notice the opportunities for growth, form a plan to take advantage of them and ask yourself: "When, where, and how will I embark on my plan?"

If things do not go the way you want or you find yourself encountering a setback, reformulate your plan and then ask yourself: "When, where, and how will I act on my new plan?" Use a consistent problem-solving focus that you can come back to again and again.

By the way, does that sound familiar? It seems that we have come full-circle in this chapter, back to the idea of deliberate practice—the strategic practice of a task over and over again until you get closer to your desired outcome.

By now you have a sense of how your current financial change project will be quite different from your previous ones. You have the tools to embark on a change journey with the right frame of mind. Now all you need are a well-defined goal and a system for monitoring your progress. Chapters three and four will help you design a goal and a tracking system.

Reflection Questions

In this chapter, you learned how Tim Brown changed a simple U-shaped curve into a "Project Mood Chart." He labeled the initial peak "hope," the valley "insight," and the final peak "confidence." Given your personal experiences with change, what three words would you use to label the U-shaped curve?

Given the financial goal that you are working on, how can you start thinking of yourself as the "doer" of an action that will facilitate your progress toward that goal? In other words, how can you make change a matter of identity?

Think about how you approach challenges in the various domains of your life (e.g., work, parenting, relationships, finances). Do your thoughts and behaviors reflect more of a fixed mindset or a growth mindset? What is one thing you could do to shift to more of a growth mindset in the realm of personal finance?

Activity

Write down potential coping thoughts you can think next time you have a bad day and cannot seem to get back on track with your financial change goal. For example, consider the following coping thoughts: "Be careful how you are judging, interpreting, or labeling your efforts. Remember that we all have setbacks. Change is a winding road. I can make tomorrow better. The fact that this is difficult means that I have taken on a worthwhile goal."

Chapter Three:
Establishing Goals and Intentions

"If you don't know where you are going, you'll end up someplace else!"

-Yogi Berra

"If you want to be happy, set a goal that commands your thoughts, liberates your energy, and inspires your hopes."

-Andrew Carnegie

Imagine that you go to bed tonight and you have a great dream. When you wake up in the morning, you can't remember the details, but you do recall a few images along with the emotional tone of the dream. You recall a particularly vivid scene where you were standing alongside a rugged coastline admiring the deep blue of the ocean and the sparkle of the sunlight on each wave. You remember feeling profoundly energized and refreshed.

The images and emotions of the dream stay with you for a few days. You develop a desire to take a restful vacation near the ocean. Living in the middle of the country, you have always been determined to head west and see the beauty of the coast. Eventually, you decide that you are going to drive from Chicago to Carmel, California, and you begin mapping out your route.

After thorough preparation, packing, and planning, you set out on your journey. Your route takes you across the Rocky Mountains—a scenic choice, but also filled with steep slopes and hairpin turns. You are thankful for the guardrails that keep your vehicle safely planted on the road. It's a long drive, but you finally reach your destination and bask in the joy of making your dream a reality.

Are you ready for a similar adventure? Such is the journey you will take as you proceed to change a financial habit. You will begin with your *dreams*. The only way to find the energy and motivation you will need for the journey is by ensuring that you are heading to an attractive destination that makes it worthwhile to expend the effort. Then you will move on to your *values*. Your values are the choices you make about what you want your life to be about. They give your dreams direction and meaning.

Next, you will create *goals*. Values and goals are two different things. Your lifelong determination to head west is a value, but the objective of getting from Chicago to Carmel is a goal. Goals are practical, obtainable outcomes that move you in valued directions. Think of your values as a compass that points you in the direction you want to move in life, and think of your goals as the essential roads and turns you highlight on the map as you prepare for your trip. The more clarity you have on your route, the more efficiently you will get to your destination.

Finally, you will design *implementation intentions*, which are the vital behaviors that are performed at crucial moments in the change journey. These vital behaviors are the guardrails that keep your car from careening off the road in the most dangerous stretches of the trip.

The order of these elements—from dreams to values to goals to implementation intentions—is essential. It wouldn't make sense to map out a trip and *then* choose the general direction you want to head. Nor would it make sense to prepare for your high-risk moments before even knowing what route you are taking. The four elements help you get progressively more specific in refining your dreams and defining the specific behaviors you would like to execute during your change venture. Let's consider each element, one at a time.

Dreams

The first step is the most fun: Allow yourself to dream. What is the future scenario that makes you most excited? Are you picturing yourself on a snowy day sitting in front of a crackling fireplace, sipping a cup of hot chocolate, secure in the knowledge that your emergency fund is so substantial that you could get snowed in for the entire winter and not have to worry about missing three months' worth of pay?

Are you picturing yourself standing atop the Haleakala Volcano in Maui, watching the sunrise, and rejoicing that you were able to save enough money to retire in Hawaii? Are you imagining the smile on a high school student's face when she realizes that she'll be able to attend the university of her choice thanks to a scholarship that you have funded?

Create a rich image of the scenes from the future that you truly, truly desire. What are the future scenarios that you want *so much* that you will do whatever it takes to get there? What makes it important enough for you to keep working on financial change despite the discomfort and hardship you will encounter?

Examples:

Olivia imagines that five years down the road, she will have launched her children from the home and given them enough money to get started in their college careers. She is able to retire and use her "bonus savings" (an account separate from her retirement savings) to travel around the country and see the National Parks.

Todd imagines that in two years, he will no longer be living paycheck to paycheck and will enjoy the security of a decent rainy-day fund. He will be saving successfully for his wedding and for a down-payment on his first home. When he pictures himself grilling hamburgers in the backyard of his home on a beautiful summer day, the image brings a smile to his face.

Allowing yourself to dream a big dream is a vital first step, because it helps you to pinpoint the financial goals that are worth all of your blood, sweat, and tears. Dreaming ensures that when you begin your change efforts, both your heart and your mind will supply you with the energy that you need to persevere.

Authors Chip Heath and Dan Heath recommend designing a "destination postcard—a vivid picture from the near-term future that shows what could be possible."[1] They explain that if you identify an inspiring destination, the rational part of yourself starts

33

figuring out how to get there, and the emotional part of yourself jumps on board. What more could you ask for?

Values

Values give your dreams direction and meaning. They reflect a range of concepts and beliefs that are important to you and that you hold dear. If your behaviors are not in line with your deepest-held values, this will create internal conflict and discomfort. If you have an understanding of what is most important to you, then you will be able to design goals that you honor and prioritize.

Here is a list of the kinds of things that people value. Read through the list and circle the ones that are most important to you. Add any of your values that are missing from the list.

Abundance	Achievement
Adventure	Attractiveness
Beauty	Comfort
Confidence	Connection with others
Creativity	Excellence
Family	Flexibility
Freedom	Friends
Fulfillment	Fun
Generosity	Growth
Happiness	Harmony
Health	Helpfulness
Hope	Independence
Influence	Knowledge
Leisure	Loyalty
Moderation	Organization
Peace of mind	Play
Popularity	Power
Responsibility	Risk

Security	Service
Simplicity	Solitude
Spirituality	Stability
Strength	Tradition
World peace	
Other:	

From the values you selected, choose your top five. Then prioritize them from most important to least important.

Sometimes our behaviors do not match with what we value most in life. Think about an area of your personal finances you would like to change. Can you think of times when your behavior in this area has conflicted with or has been inconsistent with your values?

For example, perhaps you decided that generosity is one of your core values, but you have not designed your budget in such a way to allow you to make regular donations to your favorite charity. Or perhaps you have decided that security, stability, and peace of mind are core values, but you have not established a solid emergency fund. In these examples, your behavior is inconsistent with your values. Now consider this: What do you need to do to bring your financial behavior into alignment with your values?

Consider another example. What if you are determined to save more money, but one of your highest values is enjoying pleasurable activities with your family? Perhaps you are neglecting to make regular contributions to your retirement account, opting instead to spend money on family entertainment. When it comes time to design a savings goal, it will have to be designed in such a way that it fits with your highest priorities. For example, one objective might be to spend an hour each week seeking out free, local events that your family might enjoy.

While on the topic of values, let's consider a different, somewhat tricky issue. One of the reasons why changing a behavior can be so difficult is that you may really value that behavior under a different name.

For example, you may consider yourself to have a problem with overspending, and you may pledge to modify this habit once and for all. However, maybe somewhere deep inside your brain, overspending is equated with status, free-spiritedness, freedom, or autonomy, and these are values with which you are not willing to part.

To change your overspending, then, you may need to refine your understanding of your behavior. As Ben-Shahar writes, "To be able to change, we need a nuanced understanding of what exactly it is that we want to get rid of and what we want to keep."[2] Your task is to unpackage (or "unbundle") the concept of overspending and ask yourself several questions:

- What does overspending mean to me?

- What aspects of overspending am I proud of and want to keep?

- Is there a different way for me to achieve these gains in my life without hurting myself financially? (For example, if overspending gives me a sense of autonomy, are there other ways for me to achieve autonomy that won't hurt my wallet?)

- What elements of overspending do I want to get rid of because they exact too much of a cost?

These questions will get you started in designing a goal that is truly desirable to you, without the risk of losing something else that you value.

Now let's move on to the specifics of goal setting.

Goals

After you become clear on your values, you begin to identify the route you will take on the road map that charts your path to your financial dream. Think of the AAA Travel Experts who help you plan for a road trip by marking a map with a thick yellow highlighter. They point out the essential highways, turns, and landmarks to get you to your destination with minimal confusion, construction, and roadblocks. A good financial goal will do the same.

Scientific research on goal setting has shown that goals work because they direct your attention toward goal-relevant activities, they energize you, and they lead to the discovery and use of the right strategies for the task at hand.[3] People who are successful at maintaining behavior change on a long-term basis set goals with a few basic rules in mind.

First, a good goal is specific and measurable. Edwin Locke and Gary Latham, researchers who devoted over 35 years to studying the theory of goal setting, have found that specific, challenging goals consistently lead to higher performance than nebulous goals such as "doing your best."[3] When people set out to just "do their best," goals are defined idiosyncratically and allow for a wide range of acceptable performance levels. In contrast, when goals are made specific, they reduce the ambiguity about what a person is trying to achieve, leading to fewer variations in performance.

Is your goal specific enough that everyone will agree when your goal has been reached? What exactly do you mean when you say that you aim to cut back on spending, be smarter about money, or get better at investing? Make your goals measurable and action-oriented, defining the actual behavior that you would like to see yourself perform.

Examples:

"I will have the equivalent of four months' salary in my emergency fund by the end of the year."

"I will read three books about money management in the next three months."

"I will research and then suggest to my friends two alternative activities that may replace our monthly shopping excursions."

Second, attainable goals are realistic. Do you know people who, after a large Thanksgiving feast, have pledged that they will never overeat again? Or people who have started a diet one month and committed to be three pants sizes smaller by the next month?

These vows and promises are examples of unrealistic goals that are extremely difficult to achieve. They set people up for unhealthy behavior and for feelings of discouragement and failure, which ultimately make them less motivated and confident.

How do you set a realistic goal? Don't try to change everything at once. You can always go back and adjust your goals later. And stay away from perfectionist goals that include the words "always," "never," or "every day." Perfectionist goals encourage all-or-nothing behavior. They demand perfect performance and leave no room for human error or gradual improvement. If you break a perfectionist rule, you experience defeat, leaving you with less energy to take constructive action toward your goals.

Imagine that your downfall is spending money on electronics. Rather than swearing off these purchases forever, a far more reasonable goal would be to set an annual spending limit on these items. Alternatively, you may allow yourself to buy them only in controlled circumstances (for example, after you have given yourself a three-day waiting period, compared prices in three stores, and discussed your intended purchase with a trusted friend). Ask yourself how you can make your goal realistic but still ambitious.

Third, well-designed goals are time-based. They can be broken down into a series of steps (subgoals) that are concrete, measurable, and linked to a time line. Research by Wiseman and colleagues[4] has revealed that individuals who make a step-by-step motivational plan are more likely to be successful in reaching their goals than individuals who use positive thinking and imagery. As fun as it might be to meditate upon a vision board as a means to achieving your dreams, research suggests this is not as helpful as listing detailed subgoals with a target completion date for each subgoal.

Example:

"I will have the equivalent of four months' salary in my emergency fund by the end of the year."

Subgoal 1: Fill out paperwork to arrange automatic deposit of 20% of my paycheck into my savings account. Target completion date: 02/28.

Subgoal 2: Deposit anticipated tax refund check into my savings account. Target completion date: 04/30.

Subgoal 3: Work my extra seasonal job in summer and deposit 50% of my pay into my savings account. Target completion date: 08/31.

Subgoal 4: Ride my bike to work when it is nice outside, reducing my commuting costs for at least four months. Target completion date: 12/31.

When you've designed your goal, write it down. You are more likely to achieve written goals than unwritten ones. One study even suggests that writing down your goal increases your chance of success by more than 30 percent.[5]

The findings of neuroscience support this idea. Brain researchers have discovered that neurogenesis (the birth of brain cells, or neurons) continues throughout life. They have also discovered that neurons can change themselves, their organization, and their function through new life experiences. This is known as *neuroplasticity*. If you direct your attention toward something, your attention exerts physical effects on the dynamics of the brain, and the brain starts to rewire itself to accommodate the object of your attention.[6]

When you write down your goals and then reference them again and again during your change efforts, you are repeatedly directing your attention toward your goals. This actually changes your brain to support the end outcome you desire. In contrast, if you do not write down your goals, you do not have an anchor for your attention, and this makes it less likely that a supportive brain-rewiring will occur.

It is helpful to write your goal in positive language. Describe in your goal what you are approaching, not what you are avoiding. For example, write "I will have $10,000 in my emergency savings account by the end of the year" rather than "I need to stop spending every dime when I get a paycheck."

T. Harv Eker, in his book *Secrets of the Millionaire Mind: Mastering the Inner Game of Wealth*,[7] suggests that rather than declaring "I can't afford it," replace the statement with a question: "How *can* I afford it?" Language influences our beliefs, which, in turn, influence our behaviors. Let's consider three areas of scientific research that support the idea that positive language is more effective than negative language in enhancing personal motivation.

We'll begin with the research on dispositional optimism. Individuals who are "dispositional optimists" generally expect that good things will happen in the future. They see the proverbial glass as half full (with their beverage of choice!). Their natural tendency is to make positive predictions. Studies have shown that optimists are good at maintaining their focus on reducing the discrepancy between their present behavior and a target behavior that they would like to perform in the future.[8] As a result, optimists engage in proactive behaviors to bring about greater happiness, better health, and more wealth.[9] In other words, there is a direct path from *expecting* positive outcomes to *experiencing* positive outcomes.

Next, consider the research on the cognitive model of psychotherapy. The cognitive model is one of the major schools of psychotherapy to emerge out of the twentieth century. Led by great thinkers such as Albert Ellis, Donald Meichenbaum, and Aaron Beck, psychologists discovered that our thoughts precede and determine our emotions and behaviors. Thinking negative thoughts worsens one's mood and causes a person to avoid activities that would ultimately benefit her. In contrast, thinking more balanced, coping thoughts allows a person to feel better and to remain flexible. She reduces her avoidance of activities and responds more adaptively. Again, this is evidence of a pathway from positive language to positive outcomes.

Finally, as mentioned earlier, you can use neuroplasticity in your favor. If you direct your attention toward a positive goal, you can help your brain rewire and your neurons reorganize themselves to accommodate a positive outcome. To capitalize on this effect, make a list of the benefits associated with achieving a goal, and post this list in a place where you will see it often.

Additional Considerations About Goals

At this point, you are poised to design a workable financial goal. I love the advice that the Heath brothers give in their book about change: "When you're at the beginning, don't obsess about the middle, because the middle is going to look different once you get there. Just look for a strong beginning and a strong ending and get moving."[1] It's similar to T. Harv Eker's idea that sometimes the proper sequence is "Ready, Fire, Aim!" instead of the more conservative approach.[7]

There is one last issue to consider when setting a workable goal. How high should you set the bar? Earlier in this chapter, I introduced Locke and Latham's conclusion that specific, challenging goals consistently lead to higher performance than nebulous goals such as "doing your best."[3] But how challenging should "challenging" be?

Individuals who try to answer this question seem to fall into two camps. First, there is the group who believes we should set "unreasonable goals." That is, we should set the bar excessively high as a tactic to enhance our motivation. This is the philosophy espoused by motivational speaker Les Brown in his famous quote, "Shoot for the moon. Even if you miss it, you will land among the stars." It's also the tactic adopted by strict college professors when they explain at the beginning of the semester that they do not give "A" grades, because there is no such thing as perfection. Presumably, this policy is made clear in the hopes that students will rise to the occasion and attempt to prove the professors wrong.

Timothy Ferriss, author of *The Four-Hour Workweek*,[10] places himself squarely in this camp when he urges readers to aim for unreasonable goals. He explains that individuals are more likely to succeed at goals that are nearly impossible because (1) there is less competition, and (2) such goals generate more momentum. Out of the sheer ridiculousness of setting impossible goals arises an adrenaline rush that propels you forward and helps you turn your wildest dreams into a reality.

The second camp is the group who believes that when setting goals, you should not set the bar too high lest you fail and then end up feeling defeated. Consider a scale of 0-10 where "0" represents no confidence whatsoever that you can achieve your goals, and "10" represents complete confidence that you can do it. Members of this camp believe you should set your goals at a confidence level of approximately "7." In this way, you can be fairly certain that your initial steps toward the goal will not falter, and the mastery of the first small steps may increase your drive to keep working toward the goal. According to this philosophy, if you set the bar too high, you may find the goal too overwhelming or too time-consuming and just give up.

Which camp is correct? Before I consulted the research literature, I always imagined the answer to be, "It depends." It seemed like it would depend upon one's personality, because different people are motivated in different ways. Consider the NBC hit television show *The Biggest Loser*. On the show, two groups of individuals with obesity compete to see who can lose the most weight. Two personal fitness trainers offer their expertise, advice, and support to the contestants.

In several past seasons, one of the trainers was Jillian Michaels, the tough, intense leader who yells like a drill sergeant in her effort to motivate contestants. She is not afraid of getting in people's faces or making them cry as she pushes them through a "last chance workout" before a scheduled weigh-in session.

The other trainer is Bob Harper who takes a softer, less demanding approach, attempting to uplift and nurture the contestants. He attempts to build relationships with the contestants that allow for an inner transformation, believing that this, in turn, will facilitate outward health. These training philosophies are quite different. It would seem that contestants would have a higher probability of reaching their weight loss goals if matched with the trainer who fits their personalities better.

However, the research suggests otherwise.[3,11] Numerous studies show that *the more difficult the goal, the greater the achievement*, assuming that the goal is not unrealistic, the changer is committed to the goal, and the changer has the requisite ability to achieve it.

In addition, *performance goals are strong enough variables that they mask personality differences.*

In other words, Biggest Loser contestants will be most likely to succeed if they set the bar high for their weight loss goals, and they can be reassured that their goals will be better predictors of their performance than their personality traits or preferences (or, the match or mismatch with the trainer to whom they were assigned).

What does this mean for your financial goals? It means that you would do yourself a favor by setting goals that are "unreasonable" but not unrealistic. You *should* shoot for the moon, as long as you have the tools, the ability, and the knowledge needed to get there. And your goals will be a better predictor of your future outcomes than any of the personality traits (good or bad!) you think you possess (for example, laziness, conscientiousness, or flexibility). That's a powerful argument for putting some serious thought into your goal setting.

Implementation Intentions

Patterson and colleagues, in their book *Change Anything: The New Science of Personal Success*,[12] point out that although change is difficult, it is not necessarily a 24/7 endeavor in which we are pushing ourselves to the limit at all times. Instead, we only have to focus on a handful of tempting situations when we are most at risk for regressing to our old habits. Labeled as *high-risk situations* or *crucial moments*, these are the situations that will ultimately lead us to the results we want—if only we get ourselves to do the right thing.

To find your crucial moments, look for the conditions that create the greatest temptation and threaten to take you off track as you work toward your financial goal. For example, you may have a goal of increasing your savings but find yourself straying from your budget after a stressful day at work. The late afternoon moments of feeling stressed, tired, and irritable are your crucial moments.

Alternatively, a certain environment (like a favorite shopping website or a store where there are many impulse items available) may give rise to crucial moments. Or a particular set of friends may trigger your crucial moments if they encourage you to buy things that you can't afford, or if you feel pressured to keep up with a lifestyle that is more affluent than your own.

Once you identify the scenarios that are likely to lead you astray from your goal, you need to set up specific rules that define how you should act in order to get the results you want. This process goes by various names: *scripting the critical moves,*[1] *creating vital behaviors,*[12] or *implementation intentions.*[13] An implementation intention is a highly specific plan that you will use to change your money habits at high-risk times.

Here is the basic formula to use when you are building your implementation intention:

"If I [*name the specific obstacle, such as a thought, emotion, or situation*] and I am tempted to stray from my financial goal, then I will [*choice of healthy behavior*]."

Examples:

If I drive by my favorite store on the way home from work and I am tempted to stop in and spend money, then I will stop at my favorite park instead.

If my friends invite me to a restaurant where I will end up spending beyond my means, then I will decline the invitation and offer to arrange the next gathering.

This technique is believed to work because it prompts you to identify the exact cues or triggers that lead to your unhealthy habits. This makes you more likely to notice your habitual behavior. It also makes you more likely to identify your "choice points," which are the times when you have the freedom to depart from your automatic behavior and choose something healthy for yourself.

Implementation intentions can also be used to guard against the thoughts or feelings that lead you away from goal-directed behavior:

If I experience self-disappointment and I am tempted to make myself feel better by spending money, then I will talk to a friend who always cheers me up (rather than digging a deeper financial hole!).

If I start comparing myself to my neighbors and feel tempted to spend money in order to measure up, then I will make a list of ten things in my life for which I am most grateful.

Now that you have your route planned out (goals) and your guardrails in place for the most dangerous stretches of the trip (implementation intentions), there is just one more thing to put in place before you set out for your change journey. You need a way to check the map every once in a while to make sure you are traveling in the right direction and making adequate progress. This is the idea of self-monitoring. Chapter four will address this topic. Before moving on to chapter four, spend some time on the reflection questions and activities that will help you design a financial goal and a motivational plan.

Reflection Questions

When you think about the process of designing a financial goal for yourself, are there any fears or doubts that emerge? It's good to acknowledge these. Naming your fears gives you more power over them.

Reflect upon your past efforts at goal setting, and then consider what you have learned in this chapter. What do you think will be different about your current effort to design a workable financial goal compared to what you have tried in the past?

Activities

Develop a goal and a motivational plan. Richard Wiseman, in his book *59 Seconds: Think a Little, Change a Lot*[4] suggests that to do this, you need to answer several important questions.

My overall goal is to:

What are three benefits of achieving my overall goal? List three benefits associated with your desired future.

Break your goal into five smaller steps. For each step, consider:

- The subgoal is…

- I believe that I can achieve this subgoal because…

- To achieve this subgoal, I will…

- This will be achieved by the following date…

- My reward for achieving this will be…

Reread the list of values that was presented in this chapter, and look at the values you identified in your "top five" list.

Has your financial behavior negatively impacted any of your core values? If so, how?

Which of your values provide motivation for you to change your financial behavior?

Is the financial goal that you set for yourself consistent with your highest values?

Over the course of the upcoming week, notice any of your financial behavior that *does not match with or support* your values.

Over the course of the upcoming week, notice any of your financial behavior that *supports or is consistent with* your values.

What do you need to do to bring your financial behavior into alignment with your values?

Try this exercise to "unpackage" your financial behaviors and to improve your understanding of what exactly you are trying to change.

Consider some of the financial habits or behaviors that you would like to change but have been unable to up to now (for instance, overspending, disorganization, or failure to diversify your portfolio).

Write down the aspects of each problem behavior that seem rewarding. (For example, "a sense of status when I compare myself to other people" might feel like a reward for overspending. "Not having to face the facts of my financial situation" might seem like the reward for being disorganized when it comes to your financial paperwork. Or "increased sense of stability and security" might seem like the reward for your failure to diversify your portfolio.)

Now, considering what you wrote, decide exactly what it is that you would like to change and what you would like to keep. Is there a way to attain the rewards in a healthier way, so you do not end up sabotaging your financial goals?

Chapter Four:
Self-Monitoring

"Responsibility is the price of greatness."
-Winston Churchill

Fall has arrived, and Mr. Squirrel is busy with the annual ritual of locating and burying nuts for future use. He scurries back to his dwelling inside a hole in a tree, picks up a tiny piece of chalk, and makes a tally mark on the wall of his abode. "That's fourteen acorns and one walnut," he thought. "Nuts. I must be slacking off. My records suggest that I was doing better at this time last year."

It's a ridiculous story, of course, but it raises an important point. One of the most crucial things that separates humans from animals is the ability to self-reflect; that is, humans can take themselves as the object of their attention.

This metacognitive (or, "thinking about one's thinking") ability is what allows humans to reflect upon and regulate their thoughts, emotions, and behavior. It's a powerful tool that allows humans to invest in personal growth, while squirrels and other creatures are stuck repeating the same instinctual behavior year after year. The term that describes the act of paying careful and systematic attention to a behavior that is being modified is *self-monitoring*.

Self-monitoring is a natural extension of goal setting. Once you have determined which route you will take (that is, your goal) on the road to your financial dream, you have to check the map every once in a while (self-monitoring) to make sure you are on track and on schedule. You also have to make sure you are hitting the waypoints (subgoals) along your route.

The scientific research literature hints at several important clues for how to get the most out of the work of self-monitoring. This chapter summarizes those clues. As you read this chapter, consider how you would like to design a system of self-monitoring that is tailored to your financial goal, and think about how you will implement this system as you proceed.

Remember, you have come a long way already. By now you've earned several gold stars: one for every financial change you've attempted in the past, one for obtaining this book, one for each of the first three chapters, and another for setting a workable financial goal. You owe it to yourself to design a self-monitoring system at this point so that you have a place to collect all of your future gold stars.

Functions of Self-Monitoring

Self-monitoring can serve two important functions. First, there is the pure "tracking" function, allowing an individual to notice the occurrence of a particular behavior and to produce a record of the occurrence. For example, a person might track how many times she buys coffee each month, how many times she uses her credit card for nonessential purchases during a billing cycle, or how much her net worth changes from one three-month period to another (think of net worth as a measure of the collective behaviors of saving, spending, and investing).

It can be empowering to track a behavior, because tracking reminds you of your potential for control over the behavior. The data you collect provides you with continuous immediate feedback, and it can provide a more complete and thorough account of your behavior than can be obtained by "guesstimates."

Second, there is the "change" function of self-monitoring, due to its reactive effects. *Reactivity* refers to a change in the frequency of a target behavior that is the direct result of paying attention to it. These reactive changes tend to occur in the preferred direction, with desirable behaviors increasing in frequency and undesirable behaviors decreasing in frequency.

For example, consider a person who is trying to lose weight. When she tracks exercise behavior, the duration or frequency of her physical activity will likely drift upward over time. When she tracks caloric intake, the number of calories she consumes will likely drift downward.

Now consider a person who is trying to improve the management of his finances. When he tracks how often he balances his checkbook or how often he reviews the performance of his stocks, these behaviors will increase in frequency. When he tracks how often he pays exorbitant ATM fees or how often he wastes money on lottery tickets (losing tickets, of course!), these behaviors will decrease in frequency.

Reactive effects tend to be fairly small but immediate and reliable,[1] so it is definitely worth it to take advantage of them.

<u>Capitalizing on Reactive Effects</u>

Research suggests that a number of factors influence the magnitude of reactive effects associated with self-monitoring. Korotitsch and Nelson-Gray wrote a review article about self-monitoring that summarizes these factors.[1] Here is what they found:

"In summary, based on the existing findings, a prototypical self-monitoring procedure that would maximize reactivity would be one in which (a) target responses are well-defined and motoric, (b) the client is motivated to change, (c) explicit goals for change are formulated, (d) reinforcement is provided contingent on reactive effects, (e) recordings are made just before each occurrence of the target behavior, and (f) concurrent response requirements are minimized" (p. 422).

To translate this into something useful that will help you design your own self-monitoring system, let's consider each part of the statement. First, you get better reactive effects if the behavior you are monitoring is well-defined and motoric (that is, it involves some kind of physical action, like writing). Here is an example:

- Poorly-defined target response: *I will track my financial standing.*

- Well-defined but non-motoric target response: *I will track my total net worth.*

51

- Well-defined and motoric target response: *I will fill out a written net worth tracking worksheet.*

Next, you get better reactive effects if you are motivated to change and you have set specific goals for change. Does that sound familiar? If not, you should probably go back and reread chapter three!

Korotitsch and Nelson-Gray go on to suggest that reactive effects are more likely if reinforcement or reward is provided contingent on behavior change. In other words, if you link your self-monitoring efforts with a system of rewards, you will increase the chances that your behavior will move in the desired direction.

Rewarding desired behavior is an idea that is familiar to all of us. We use it quite commonly when we are attempting to change a health behavior. For instance, a woman who is trying to lose weight might reward herself with a new piece of clothing when the results of the weekly weigh-in are favorable. A man who is cutting back on smoking might put all of the money he would otherwise be spending on cigarettes into a jar, and then when the funds are sufficient, take an exotic vacation.

It is possible to sabotage your change behavior by choosing the wrong reward. It would be self-defeating, for instance, to reward yourself with a box of Krispy Kreme doughnuts in celebration of the fact that you lost ten pounds.

This is a trap that people fall into quite easily in the financial domain. For an individual who is trying to be cautious about spending, the self-sabotaging thought process might sound something like this: "I deserve that new big-screen TV; my checkbook ledger shows how hard I've been working." Alternatively, the reasoning might be: "I made so many financial sacrifices this month; I can reward myself with a shopping trip."

For most people (although there are exceptions), when trying to set up a reward system for a financial behavior change, it is best to choose rewards that are free or low-cost. Consider all of the healthy pleasures that have been found to have a measurable, positive effect on our well-being.[2] Whether it is enjoying nature, laughter, social connection, or a nap, choose rewards that are meaningful and valuable to you, and avoid rewards that will take you farther away from your goal.

Another factor to consider when setting up a self-monitoring system is how often you will make a recording of your behavior. The research suggests that reactive effects are greater when you record each occurrence of a target behavior, rather than just recording every second or third occurrence or using a random recording schedule.

Think about your checkbook register. If you are faithful about making entries into the register every time you write a check or use your debit card, you get instant feedback about the amount of money in your account. It directs your focus to the change in your account balance. It draws your attention to the consequences of making that particular expenditure. You are more likely to be careful, then, when considering your next purchase.

However, if you only balance your checkbook once a month or you just check your account balance on an occasional bank statement, *you have more psychological distance from the consequences of your spending behavior*. It is easy, then, to lose sight of both your account balance and your money management goal.

According to research, not only should you record each occurrence of the target behavior, but you should try to make that recording just *before*, rather than after, the target response. For example, in one study, individuals who smoked cigarettes were instructed to record smoking behavior just before its occurrence. The reactive effects then increased, and they were able to reduce their cigarette consumption.[3] Similarly, in another study, individuals who were trying to lose weight were more successful when they were instructed to record food intake before eating.[4]

In the financial domain, you can put this piece of wisdom into practice by starting the entry in your check register before you even make it to the cash register in the store. This would draw your attention to your account balance and give you a chance to reevaluate the purchase in light of your financial goals.

Korotitsch and Nelson-Gray listed one more factor that influences the magnitude of reactive effects associated with self-monitoring.

They wrote that "concurrent response requirements" should be minimized. In other words, when you are trying to monitor multiple behaviors at the same time, the reactive effects are decreased. However, if you focus on consistent tracking of one target behavior, your behavior is more likely to drift in the desired direction.

Making Self-Monitoring Concrete

Remember the toy cash registers they used to make for children? They were brightly colored, had lots of buttons to push, and usually had play money (plastic coins and paper bills) for children to count and sort.

It seems that sometime between my own childhood and the present day, toy cash registers have become a lot more complex, offering make-believe cashiers the option of accepting credit or debit from their pretend customers. Many of these modern toys are promoted for preschool-aged children. Considering that credit and debit are abstract concepts, and children typically do not reach the stage of cognitive development to understand abstract concepts until much later in childhood, it is hard to believe that young ones could even grasp the idea of credit and debit. In contrast, play cash is something that kids can touch and move and count, and it is much easier for their young brains to comprehend.

In the same way, when it comes to adults who are trying to reign in their spending, it is easier to monitor the use of cash than the use of credit. Economics professor Robert Frank from Cornell University appeared as a guest on National Public Radio's Morning Edition in July 2008 and was interviewed by Ari Shapiro.[5] Frank indicated that "...parting with [cash] is just a more vivid sensation than the abstract act of signing a pledge to pay something later in the future."

He went on to cite a statistic that when McDonald's restaurants starting accepting credit cards from customers to pay for their fast-food purchases, the average purchase went from $4.50 to $7.00. This demonstrates that people do not keep track of their money as closely when using plastic. Cash is a concrete object that you can manipulate and count, and the tangible nature of cash makes it more conducive to self-monitoring for individuals who aim to reduce spending.

Another way to make your self-monitoring more concrete is to take advantage of websites that are designed to help you visualize debt. For instance, Kyle Reiach has designed a website called therealdamage.com. The site allows you to learn how much your money would "really" be worth if you used it to pay off a piece of your debt instead of purchasing a coveted item. Another of Reiach's websites is daystopay.com, which calculates how long you need to work to pay for something you want.

Reiach and others like him are trying to help us out because they realize how easy it is to get lost in abstract numbers in the financial world. For example, life can get confusing when we compare interest rates, shop for investment products, and consider insurance policies, because so many of these are described in the abstract.

When making financial decisions or engaging in self-monitoring, it is helpful to translate figures into a concrete or tangible value that is easier to grasp than a number. For example, if an individual is deciding whether it is worth it to try to keep some of her money in an interest-earning checking account or whether it would be acceptable to spend it each month, she might think about the value of one month's accrued interest as a tangible product—like one tank of gas or one bag of groceries.

If you are monitoring the performance of an investment vehicle or an insurance product over time, you might compare the long-term value of your investment to the short-term value of immediate purchases. Then, you can understand your financial achievements in terms of a concrete value.

For example, "The money that I used to purchase one share of stock one year ago could have purchased dinner for two and the temporary satisfaction of a full stomach. Now, I still have the money, plus the value of it has grown by the equivalent of two fancy beverages at my favorite coffee shop. Additionally, I acquired the knowledge of how this stock tends to perform, as well as the potential for continued growth well into the future."

Section Summary

By now, you have learned how important it is to prepare for the change process with the proper frame of mind. You have put time and thoughtful reflection into your financial goal setting. You have learned that a good self-monitoring system will serve a tracking function and may even boost personal change. You are now ready to begin working toward your goal.

In the next section, you will learn about some of the most powerful change technologies that social science has to offer. Best wishes as you continue your journey.

Reflection Questions

Have you ever changed the frequency of one of your habits or behaviors simply by paying closer attention to that behavior?

In the past, what has made your self-monitoring efforts easier or more difficult? How might you get around any obstacles or barriers that emerge as you monitor your progress toward your financial goal?

Activity

Design a system of tracking or self-monitoring that you will use to boost your personal change efforts as you work through the remaining chapters of this book.

Section II

Chapter Five:
Stages of Change

"It's not that some people have willpower and some don't. It's that some people are ready to change and others are not."

-James Gordon

Which of the following people is most likely to succeed in completing a marathon? Person A believes that if you can walk somewhere, walking beats running hands-down, every single time. Person B can think of a million reasons why participating in a marathon would be a good idea, but he can think of an equal number of reasons why it would take too much effort.

Person C signed up for the marathon, but he hasn't purchased his athletic shoes yet. He also hasn't researched the type of terrain on which he will be running. So far, all of his running experience has been in his backyard (thankfully, it's a really big yard). Person D signed up, did his homework, and faithfully executed an appropriate training run every morning for the past several months.

It's obvious that Person D has the best shot of crossing the finish line in the near future. We would describe him as being in the "action stage of change" with regard to the goal of completing a marathon. It doesn't mean that Persons A, B, and C are failures. It doesn't mean that they won't eventually get there. It simply means that they are in different states of readiness for taking on this goal.

Before you embark on a journey of personal change, it is helpful to have a sense of your *stage of change* or *state of readiness for change*. The stages of change hold important clues about what resources are needed to create forward movement toward a goal. If you know your stage of change, it will help you design appropriate self-challenges or change tasks. These change tasks allow you to focus your energy, optimize your problem-solving efforts, and avoid exerting yourself on actions that are *not* going to help you make progress.

This chapter describes the stages of change, also known as the transtheoretical model[1], and helps you apply it to your financial goal.

History

In the 1970's, a researcher by the name of James Prochaska became interested in change. In particular, he wanted to categorize all of the different types and processes of human change. He decided to look closely at several different theories of psychotherapy to identify the major themes that emerged.

Then, he and his colleagues, John Norcross and Carlo DiClemente, set out to study more than 1,000 people who were considered to be "successful self-changers." They believed that the key to fostering personal change lay in the experience of the people who were able to initiate and maintain change on their own. Out of their efforts grew a six-stage model that describes the pathway to habit modification.

The model was first applied to individuals who were attempting to break the habit of substance abuse or addictions. Then, further study revealed that the model had equal utility when it was applied to health behavior change in general (for example, quitting smoking, starting an exercise program, or reducing portion sizes). Eventually, the model was applied to multiple other domains of human functioning.

A key idea of the model is that if you want to modify a habit, you benefit from knowing your current stage of readiness for the problem at hand. Then, you can match the proper challenges, tasks, or "homework" to your current stage of change. This will allow you to maintain motivation, turn setbacks into progress, and maximize the effectiveness of your personal change efforts.

The Six Stages

So what are the stages of change? Stage one (precontemplation) is when *a person is not particularly interested in changing and does not want to learn more about her problem.* Other people may want her to change, but she has no intention to change in the near future.

Consider an organization where the employer matches workers' contributions to the employer-sponsored retirement plan. Now think of a woman who works at such an organization but fails to take advantage of the match. Her coworkers encourage her to tap this benefit, but she gets defensive and wonders why they have to make such a big deal out of it. She really doesn't want to hear about the potential consequences of ignoring the match. Her denial is a good example of stage one behavior.

Stage two (contemplation) is when *a person feels strongly pulled in two different directions.* On the one hand, he can name several of the potential benefits of change. On the other hand, he is acutely aware of the costs associated with change. In this stage, procrastination and feelings of ambivalence are common.

Imagine a man who is thinking about getting rid of his cable service as a way to cut down on monthly expenses. He makes a list of reasons why this is a good idea: (1) he'd have more money to put in his savings; (2) it would ease the monthly struggle of figuring out how to cover all of the bills; and (3) too much TV is bad for your brain, anyway.

Then, he makes a list of reasons why he isn't ready to give up the cable: (1) Monday Night Football; (2) Jersey Shore; and (3) keeping up with the neighbors, all of whom have cable TV. When the list-making is complete, he realizes that the two sides balance themselves out perfectly, and he is left teetering between the two choices. It feels like torture when he tries to make a decision, and so he puts it off. Such is the dilemma faced by people in stage two. If the procrastination goes on too long, individuals get stuck in this stage and become "chronic contemplators."

Stage three (preparation) is when *a person intends to take action soon, but she needs to get all of her ducks in a row and to make a specific plan of action.* By the time a person reaches this stage, she has resolved the ambivalence of the previous stage. The balance has tipped solidly in the direction of change. Before jumping into action, though, she needs to work out the logistics of change.

For example, consider a woman who plans to live on a new household budget. She runs the numbers, devises a couple of versions of a budget, and consults with other members of the household before choosing a plan. Her energy is invested in taking the small steps she believes will help her make the new budget a success.

Stage four (action) is when *a person has started changing his behavior and needs to work hard to keep moving forward.* When he has been successful with the new behavior for approximately six months, he moves into the next stage.

In stage five (maintenance), *a person tries to become aware of situations or conditions that might tempt him to slip back into his old behavior patterns, and he learns how to cope with these temptations in a healthy way.*

Finally, in stage six (termination), *the individual has complete confidence in his new, healthy behavior and feels certain that he will not return to his old, unhealthy habit.*

Relapse

Another concept that is a part of this model is that of relapse (or "recycling"), which is not one of the stages of change, but is *a return from the action or maintenance stage to an earlier stage.*

When Prochaska and his colleagues interviewed successful self-changers as a part of their initial research, they soon discovered that many self-changers had to cycle through the various stages several times before making the new behavior stick. For instance, they found that most people who quit smoking recycled their efforts three or four times before succeeding. And most people who mastered a New Year's resolution had to make the resolution for five consecutive years before reaching the maintenance stage of change.[2]

As common as relapse and recycling are, it is good to remember that you *learn* something every time you make a trip around the wheel of change. When you experience a setback in your change journey, it often feels like you are going in circles rather than solving your problem. You might even say that you feel like you are "back at square one." In actuality, every time you circle around the wheel of change, you end up in a place that is one level higher than your previous starting point because you learned something from your effort.

In this view, it is really a "spiral of change" rather than a flat circle of change.[2] If you think of yourself as being part of a change spiral, there is less justification for feelings of defeat, disappointment, hopelessness, and frustration. You can look for the lessons you learned from your trip around the spiral, and you will not experience the negative feelings that can trigger or sustain a relapse.

You may have noticed that the idea of a change spiral is similar to the idea of the "growth mindset" that you learned about in chapter two. To make things simple, keep in mind that this basic rule of thumb can buffer you against discouragement: *Everything is hard before it is easy, and relapse is simply a normal sign that you are moving up the spiral of change*. This reminder can make a tremendous difference to your level of motivation.

Pause for Thought

It's time to be brutally honest with yourself. At this point, take a closer look at your newly-designed financial goal. What is your starting point? What is your current stage of change with regard to your goal? Because you have identified an issue or problem that needs to be addressed and you are reading this book, you are probably *not* in stage one.

Are you in stage **two** (contemplation), vacillating between moving forward and maintaining the status quo? If you hear yourself saying that you are "stuck" or "lazy," this is an important clue that you may be in stage two. If you think to yourself, "I just can't find the motivation," this is another hint.

Many of us think that motivation is something that hides from us, if only we could search in the right place. Off we go on a quest to find this elusive virtue. In the framework of the stages of change model, though, motivation is not something you have to *find* before you do the work of change. Instead, "I can't seem to get motivated" is interpreted to mean "I am not fully ready for change." And if *that's* the case, there are still plenty of relevant change tasks for you. These tasks are likely to involve mental work instead of physical action, but they are effective change tasks nonetheless.

The best image to represent the contemplation stage is that of a balance (remember that from high school chemistry class?). Imagine that one pan holds the "pros of change," while the other pan holds the "cons of change."

From day to day or from moment to moment, the pans swing back and forth. First one side weighs more, then the other. You can only move past the contemplation stage when you do something that will forever make the "pros" weigh more than the "cons." Many of the readers of this book may be in the contemplation stage, facing this exact challenge.

Perhaps you have already moved on to stage **three** (preparation). You are about to begin work on your change project, but you have to get all of the details in place first. The best image to represent the preparation stage is that of "ducks in a row."

Imagine that you are a mother duck, and you are getting ready for the adventures of a spring day with your newly-hatched ducklings. You know that your brood needs to get to the pond down the street for their first swimming lesson, but you also know that some of your ducklings are quite curious, courageous, and adventurous. Left to their own devices, they may not get to today's destination. Your job, then, is to get all of the ducks in a row and to have plans in place to deal with distractions that may tempt your little ones to stray from the line. Does this sound like the challenge you are facing? You may be in the preparation stage.

Some readers may feel they are already in the action stage of change (stage **four**). They may think to themselves, "I have already taken steps to get this change going, so I am in action." If this describes you, answer the following questions:

- Have you made a strong commitment to change?

- Are you willing to work hard and make sacrifices to ensure success?

- Have you come to a realization that there are no simple solutions to your problem, and that your old methods will not get you new results?

- Have you completed a thorough and systematic period of preparation, laying all of the groundwork for your new behavior?

If you can answer "yes" to all of these questions, you are indeed in the action stage of change. If you answered "no" to one or more of the questions, you are still doing the mental work of an earlier stage (two or three).

It is perfectly OK to be in stage two or three. *You are far more likely to be a successful changer if you accept your true starting point and work on the relevant change tasks than if you pretend to be in a later stage (and therefore use the wrong set of tasks)*. In other words, the biggest favor that you can do for yourself is to be honest about your true starting point.

Research suggests that many people succumb to something called the *above average effect* (otherwise known as *superiority bias* or *positive illusions*) when they are sizing up their assets and abilities. The above average effect is a bias in thinking that causes some individuals to overestimate their positive qualities and underestimate their negative qualities, relative to other people. For example, 93% of adults in the U.S. estimate that their driving skills are in the top 50%.[3] Many people overestimate their intelligence, popularity, relationship satisfaction, and participation in healthy activities.

Many individuals fall prey to this bias, as well, when they are reflecting on their financial standing or when they are estimating their starting point for a financial goal. See if you can challenge yourself to be bold and daring and to fight the superiority bias when identifying your current stage of change. Make sure you are brutally honest with yourself about the status of your recent goal-related efforts. If it helps, invite a trusted friend to help you evaluate your true starting point with regard to your financial goal.

A Common Mismatch

Imagine that you have just moved to a new town and you want to get established with a new financial adviser. You open up the phone book, flip to the right section, and find that you have two choices (OK, so you probably didn't move to New York City!). You really want to make the right choice, so you decide to interview both professionals in person. Adviser A really "wows" you. She does a quick assessment of your financial situation and whips together a detailed financial action plan that is custom-designed for you. The plan has a list of recommended steps for you to take based on the latest and greatest information about wealth management.

Adviser B, on the other hand, tells you that she would like to spend some time gathering your thoughts about the obstacles that have interfered with your financial goals in the past. In addition, she would like to learn more about your fundamental values and whether your financial choices tend to support or conflict with your value system. In other words, she would really like to understand what your money choices mean to you before you create an action plan together.

Which adviser is the better choice? Of course, it depends on your current stage of change with regard to the financial goals that you are bringing to your appointment. Adviser A assumes you are in the action stage of change (stage four). In fact, most personal finance books, wealth management seminars, financial gurus, and advisers assume that the whole audience is in the action stage.

The reality, though, is that many members of the audience are in earlier stages of change. Unfortunately, this sets up a mismatch between the message that is being delivered (an "action" message) and the message that the audience is actually ready for (one that helps them develop greater awareness of the problem or engage in a thoughtful period of preparation).

That is why many action plans fall short. If individuals are prompted to begin with the change tasks that are most effective in the action stage without having first gained awareness and readiness in the earlier stages (stages two and three), change is not likely to stick. As Prochaska, Norcross, and DiClemente explain, "Overt action without insight is likely to lead to temporary change."[2]

Adviser B seems to be a good fit for an individual who is in the contemplation stage of change (stage two). She is interested in helping her clients do the mental work of linking their behaviors with their value system, thereby shifting the balance in the direction of change once and for all. Many people may believe they are accomplishing more by choosing Adviser A over Adviser B, but if you are trying to execute an action plan before laying the foundation, your goals will be on unstable ground.

All of this is an argument for the value of slowing down the change process and being more reflective (and as a result, more accurate) about the proper pathway toward a goal. At the end of this chapter, there will be reflection questions and activities to assist you with this important undertaking. Before you get to that, let's take a look at the change tasks associated with each stage of change.

Change Tasks

After you determine your true starting point with regard to your financial goal, it is time to learn how to propel yourself forward. You can now identify the "homework," self-challenges, or change tasks that will help you create movement from one stage of change to another. Remember that the change tasks you will use to move from stage one to stage two are *different* from the change tasks you will use to move from stage two to stage three, and so forth.

Matching your change homework to your current stage of change will help you maximize your problem solving efforts and increase the chances of success. It might be tempting to jump into the work of the action stage, but you will not be able to sustain action unless you have completed the work of the earlier stages.

If your starting point is stage one, your primary task is to become more open-minded and less defensive about the possibility of changing a specific behavior. For example, if you have been getting feedback from the universe about the need to change something (stop buying lottery tickets, stop opening new credit cards, start contributing to your employer-sponsored retirement fund, and so on) and you have been doing everything in your power to block out this feedback, the first step is to *stop resisting and simply observe.*

See if you can identify the walls that you put up to avoid thinking about change. Are you in denial about the consequences of a particular habit? Are you aware of the consequences but prone to minimizing them or explaining them away?

Next, see if you can gather information that will allow you to open up to the possibility of changing your behavior. For instance, can you find out how big the problem is if you refuse to make contributions to your 401(k)? Can you calculate the total sum of how much you spend on lottery tickets per year? No need to make a decision to change at this point. You are just trying to look around, see what other people do, and see why other people think your current behavior might be problematic.

Eventually, you can speculate why you do what you do and pinpoint which defenses are getting in the way of healthier behavior. You'll know you have completed this stage when you are able to check your defenses at the door and openly consider the possibility of change.

If your starting point is stage two, your homework involves both "thinking tasks" and "feeling tasks." On the thinking side of things, your job is to expand your awareness of your problem behavior by monitoring how your thoughts maintain the problem. Consider completing a *decisional balance* exercise in which you create a two-by-two grid. The rows are labeled "pros" and "cons," and the columns are labeled "changing" and "not changing." When you fill in each square of the grid, take the time to consider the consequences of changing versus not changing to yourself and to others.

On the feeling side of things, your job is to get your emotions involved in your change efforts. In most change situations, you have to be able to see the problem in ways that influence your feelings, not just your thoughts. Very often, if you can't find an aspect of the problem that impacts you at the emotional level, you can't find the drive or the energy for change. The homework, then is to imagine what the future will be like if you do NOT succeed at personal change. Attempt to paint a grim picture of the future that will shift the balance in the direction of change. Key questions to ask yourself include:

- What will happen if I continue along my current path?

- What will my future look like if I do NOT make progress in this area?

- What aspects of my problem generate feelings of disappointment, disgust, or distress inside of me?

- How much power and control does my problem behavior have over me, and what positive things am I missing in my life because of it?

- What positive things will I miss out on in the future because I am refusing to change this behavior in the present?

- How do I fail myself by refusing to change this habit?

After you've painted a detailed picture of the future that focuses on the negative aspects of the problem, design a forward-looking appraisal of how much healthier and happier life will be when you have completed a change. Imagine how you will think and feel about yourself after you change. Picture yourself feeling good about your habits because your behavior is now aligned with your deepest values.

The practice of creating two very different future scenarios, one negative and one positive, is known as *mental contrasting*. When you use this technique, you can't help but notice the gap between the two scenes. The gap creates discomfort or distress (known in psychology as *cognitive dissonance*). There is a feeling of tension when you hold two conflicting thoughts or images in your head simultaneously, and you become motivated to resolve the discrepancy. In this case, you get relief from the discomfort when you make a firm decision to change your financial behavior.

You'll know you have completed this stage when you have developed a personal conviction about the value of change and the need for change. Most importantly, at this point, you have made a decision to pursue change. You have done something to resolve your former ambivalence and to forever make the "pros" of change outweigh the "cons."

If your starting point is stage three, you will focus on making a plan for the future and solidifying your commitment to change. You can start by making a list of the benefits of change and keeping it with you wherever you go. For example, if you are attempting to save more money, write a brief list of the reasons you are saving (the reasons that have the biggest emotional impact) and put copies of it in crucial places like the inside of your wallet and the side of your computer monitor.

Your next step is to create a strong, positive image of your future self. Key questions to ask yourself include:

- After I have been successful in making this change, how will my thoughts be different? My feelings? My behavior?

- What will my new behavior free me up to achieve or become?

- In what ways will my life be enhanced once I have mastered this change?

To solidify your commitment to change, set a date that you think is a reasonable date to launch your change plan. Make your commitment public. As you learned in the chapter on goal setting, public commitments are more powerful than private pledges because they enhance your sense of accountability and may help you garner social support for your efforts.

Prochaska, Norcross, and DiClemente advise that in the preparation stage, you should prepare for your change efforts in much the same way that you would prepare for a major operation or medical procedure. This means putting your change plan first, and making everything else in your life second.

Anticipate and prepare for the fact that your mood, your relationships with family and friends, and your daily functioning may change as you shift your energy and focus toward your change efforts. For example, if you plan to eliminate the daily flavored latte from your diet (in the service of saving $28 per week), you may want to warn your coworkers in advance about a possible change in your energy level and functioning!

Consider another example. If you will be allocating more of your paycheck toward your tax-sheltered annuity, you may have less money to take your family on vacation. This could have consequences for your family's overall level of stress. Before this happens, you may wish to sit down with your family members and brainstorm alternative ways to renew yourselves and reconnect.

Create a concrete plan of action. What specific steps will you take to reach your goal? What obstacles or barriers may arise that you will have to overcome? Make a list of all of the strategies you will use to cope with anticipated barriers to change.

Remember implementation intentions from chapter three? They are a great strategy to use during the preparation stage. Your job is to identify the conditions that will create the greatest temptation and threaten to take you off track as you work toward your goal. Then design a specific rule that defines how you will act under those conditions.

Enlist the support of the important people in your life. Share your change plan with them and tell them specifically how they can be most helpful to you. You'll know you have completed the preparation stage when you have made a firm commitment to a detailed action plan.

If your starting point is stage four, your primary task is to execute your action plan. In this stage, do everything you can to set yourself up for success. Make good use of the strategies you will learn in the following chapters on self-efficacy, persistence, and impulse control. Maximize your social support by providing a written self-change contract to all of your helpers and asking them to provide rewards for specific types of progress.

You'll know you have completed the action stage when you have consistently executed your new habit for approximately six months, and your new behavior now feels less effortful and more automatic.

The individual who successfully completes the action stage moves on to the maintenance stage. There is a whole chapter devoted to the topic of maintenance later in this book. For now, congratulate yourself on mastering another change concept, and take some time to reflect on the following questions.

Reflection Questions

Is it hard for you to be honest with yourself about your true starting point for change with regard to your specific financial goal? If so, what makes it hard? How can you make it "OK" to accept your current stage of change?

Have you ever encountered a mismatch between a message that was delivered to you (perhaps by a financial adviser or a self-help guide) and the message that you were actually *ready* for? If so, what stage of change did the speaker or author assume you were in? What stage of change were you actually in? What message would have been a better fit for your stage of readiness?

Activity

List the change tasks that correspond to your current stage of change. Then specify how you can apply each of these change tasks to your specific financial goal.

Chapter Six:
Self-Efficacy

"In order to succeed, people need a sense of self-efficacy, strung together with resilience to meet the inevitable obstacles and inequities of life."

–Albert Bandura

"Whether you think you can or think you can't—you are right."

–Henry Ford

I have seen no better movie about personal change than *The King's Speech*,[1] which won the Academy Award for "Best Picture" in 2011. The movie is the story of Albert, the Duke of York, who suddenly became King George VI of the United Kingdom and was forced to confront his life-long struggle with stuttering.

His speech therapist, Lionel Logue, employed a number of creative strategies to help the king improve his speech and, perhaps more importantly, overcome fear. In the movie, the king made a transformation from a hesitant, self-doubting, temperamental man to a capable and more confident king.

The film is a great illustration of several important change strategies, many of which are described in this book. For example, it shows the main character making personal change a matter of identity and allowing emotion to be a powerful motivator that supports his efforts. It also shows him making use of social support at the moments when he feels discouraged or hesitant.

Most importantly for this chapter, the film is a great illustration of the concept of *self-efficacy*, which is a concept that lies at the heart of psychologist Albert Bandura's social cognitive theory.[2-3] Self-efficacy is *the belief in one's ability to organize and carry out the courses of action necessary to achieve a goal or manage a situation.* Persons who have a strong sense of self-efficacy devote their attention and effort to the demands of a given situation or challenge. They rise to the occasion, because they believe they have what it takes to reach their end goal.

The movie portrayed the king developing this belief in himself and his resources, enough so that by the end of the film he was able to deliver an important public address with minimal intrusion of his speech impediment. Later in this chapter, we'll take a look at the factors that enhance one's sense of self-efficacy, borrowing examples from the film. First, let's find out how self-efficacy impacts our performance.

Influence of Self-Efficacy

According to Bandura, people who think of themselves as highly efficacious tend to think, feel, and act differently from those who perceive themselves as inefficacious.[3] In one of Bandura's famous quotes, he states that people who think of themselves as efficacious "produce their own future, rather than simply foretell it."[4] Research shows that this personal belief influences the choices people make, the effort they put forth in working toward a goal, how long they persist when confronted with obstacles, and how they feel in the process of working toward goals.

Imagine that your goal is to become well-versed in the language of finance and investment. You want to know how to evaluate the health and resiliency of a public company by inspecting its quarterly earnings report. Also, you want to understand what it means when the announcer on the radio states that a public company "missed Wall Street estimates by five cents."

If you have a strong sense of self-efficacy with regard to this goal, you choose to visit the finance/business section of the bookstore rather than restricting your browsing to the usual sections where you feel most comfortable. You set aside time to educate yourself about finance and investment, perhaps an hour or two every weekend, even though you would rather be relaxing or catching up on things around the house.

When obstacles arise in your path, you persist in working around them. If a chapter you are reading is above your level of comprehension, you read it over and over again until you understand it. Or, you ask a friend or family member to help you understand it.

Your default setting is to expose yourself to as many opportunities as you can that will help you reach your goal. If it takes listening to "Marketplace Money" from American Public Media every night on the radio during your drive home from work, then so be it. Although you certainly feel frustrated and overwhelmed at times, overall you feel a sense of curiosity, excitement, determination, and pride.

On the other hand, if you have a weak sense of self-efficacy with regard to this goal, you are not necessarily going to make choices that support your goal. "Let's see, should I read the business section of the newspaper or the comics? That's easy—comics!" You are not willing to invest too much time or effort in pursuing your goal.

If you read a book on investing and it seems too difficult or too time-consuming, you are quick to set the book down and shift to an activity that feels less taxing. When obstacles arise, you make excuses or rationalize why you cannot pursue your goal at this time. When you do try to work toward your goal, your dominant emotions are discouragement, frustration, anxiety, or even hopelessness.

In general, a strong sense of self-efficacy with regard to a particular goal creates the framework that allows you to take advantage of the resources and activities that move you along the path to successful change. Think of it as a self-fulfilling prophecy: *If you believe you have what it takes, you will create the circumstances in which you do, indeed, have what it takes to reach your target.*

Enhancing Self-Efficacy

The 64-million dollar question, then, is this: What happens if you measure the strength of your self-efficacy on the efficacy-o-meter, and it comes up "weak?" Is there a way to strengthen this psychological resource in the service of a specific goal? Thankfully, the answer is "yes." Your sense of self-efficacy can be enhanced when you are successful in taking small steps toward your goal or when you learn to associate positive feelings with your new behavior.

More specifically, Bandura identified four conditions that augment self-efficacy: (1) mastery experiences, (2) modeling, (3) verbal persuasion, and (4) stress management. If you capitalize on these four conditions, it will support your momentum toward your money goals. Let's consider each one in turn.

Mastery Experiences

In *The King's Speech*, the speech therapist who worked with the king made an important observation early in their work together. He noticed that the king felt demoralized and hopeless with regard to the possibility of correcting his speech. The king repeated pessimistic utterances such as "I can't" and "No one can fix it."

The speech therapist was astute enough to realize that the king needed to experience an "early success" in order to reverse the feelings of hopelessness and strengthen his commitment to treatment. Therefore, he engineered a situation in which the king could hear a recording of himself reading a passage aloud with no stuttering. Sure enough, when the king played the recording, it prompted his decision to return to the speech therapist's office for further treatment, even though he had previously given up and stormed out.

This is a good illustration of the importance of *mastering a small step* or *engineering an early win*. When you experience a sense of mastery over a small step, your feelings of hopelessness are converted into reassurance. You build confidence that you can, indeed, make forward progress toward your goal because after all, you have already conquered part of it.

Chip and Dan Heath call this strategy "shrinking the change."[5] They indicate that when you are facing a daunting task that you are tempted to avoid, you should carve out a small enough piece of that change so that you can't help but score a victory. They suggest that the emotional side of yourself needs fuel to keep trudging along on the change journey, and the boost that you get from "small wins" is an important source of that fuel.

The Heath brothers refer to a paper written by psychologist Karl Weick entitled "Small Wins: Redefining the Scale of Social Problems."[6] In the paper, Weick describes the purpose of a small win this way: "A small win reduces importance ('this is no big deal'), reduces demands ('that's all that needs to be done'), and raises perceived skill levels ('I can do at least that')." These three factors combine to help you replace feelings of dread with confidence and hope.

Now back to your money goal. How can you engineer a small success early on in order to strengthen your belief in yourself and your personal resources? If your goal is to build a rainy-day fund by the end of the year, what is a small step you can take today? Can you go to the bank and open an account that will be your designated emergency fund? If that is too big of a leap, can you go online and research the banks and credit unions in your area to decide where you would like to establish an account?

If your goal is to rebalance your 401(k) account but you have no clue where to start, what is a small step you can take today? Can you make a trip to the library to find a book about how to evaluate mutual fund performance? Can you make a phone call to your uncle, the financial analyst, to ask him for his thoughts? Remember to choose an action that is within easy reach. In this way, you can experience immediate reinforcement.

Modeling

There is a humorous scene in *The King's Speech* in which the king tricks Lionel, the speech therapist, into revealing to his wife that Albert is his client. Lionel was clearly not ready to share this with his wife for fear that she would be angry at him for keeping such a secret. It was an interesting maneuver because it allowed Albert to watch his therapist overcome his fear and accomplish something challenging. It was as if the king, knowing that he needed to overcome his own fears, wanted to watch someone model this behavior for him.

If you see someone who is similar to you struggling with a similar problem and then making progress toward overcoming that problem, this will increase your confidence that you can overcome it, as well. In Bandura's model, this is known as *vicarious experience* or *modeling*. Research reveals that this source of information is somewhat weaker than mastery experiences in helping to strengthen self-efficacy beliefs. However, when you are uncertain about your abilities or when you have limited prior experience with a given task, vicarious experience can help quite a bit.

Vicarious experience is particularly powerful when you perceive the model to be similar to you on relevant dimensions or attributes. For instance, in the movie, there is a scene in which Winston Churchill reveals to Albert that he, too, once had a speech impediment that he had worked to overcome. It must have been comforting for Albert to realize that another high-ranking member of society had fought a similar battle. Had a low-ranking servant shared that he had overcome a speech deficit, the information may not have had the same impact on the king. Observing the success of someone who is like you allows you to conclude, "If he can do it, then so can I!"

You can strengthen your sense of self-efficacy for your money goal by observing someone who is similar to you making progress toward a similar financial goal. Imagine that I am looking for a good role model to help me strengthen my sense of self-efficacy for becoming a successful investor. Perhaps I am choosing between Donald Trump, Suze Orman, and one of my coworkers.

After some investigation, I realize that I have almost nothing in common with Donald Trump, the American business magnate whose father was a real-estate developer and self-made millionaire. Donald learned many of his investment skills by working in his father's real estate company after college. I am not aware of any self-made millionaires in my family (unless they are holding out!). I simply cannot relate to that, nor am I likely to have similar opportunities arise in my life in the future.

Moving on to Suze Orman, the financial adviser, motivational speaker, and television host who is famous for empowering women to be financially savvy: I have a bit more in common with her. She is a woman who grew up in a working class family, she has a mental health background (a Bachelor's degree in social work), and at the age of 30, she was still a waitress making $400 a month. I was actually making more than that at age 30, but my net worth at that time definitely looked more like that of a waitress than a real estate tycoon. Suze, then, might be a better source of vicarious learning for me.

Finally, considering a hypothetical third choice, imagine that I have a coworker who grew up in a similar socioeconomic background and who is just a few years ahead of me on the career trajectory. She does the same job I do and has similar income and benefits. Just a few years ago, she decided that she needed to educate herself about the world of investment in order to know what she is doing with her retirement accounts.

If I observe her making good progress toward this goal, she might be the best possible model for me to choose. Her situation is clearly the closest to mine. As an added bonus, she is easily accessible to me, assuming that she is willing to discuss her financial experiences. This coworker will help me strengthen my sense of self-efficacy for my goal of becoming a successful investor.

Verbal Persuasion

The people in your life can help you strengthen your sense of self-efficacy by acting as role models. If they cannot do that, a different role they can play is to offer *verbal persuasion*. There were many people who were willing to offer encouraging statements to Albert in *The King's Speech*. They assured him that he would "make a fine king" and that he would be "splendid" when delivering his speech. True to the research in this area, Albert could only accept these encouraging statements when they were delivered from an individual whom he considered to be genuine and trustworthy and whom he perceived to truly understand the demands of the task at hand.

If you receive encouraging verbal feedback from someone whom you trust, this will increase your sense of self-efficacy for the task you face. To be effective, the verbal feedback should persuade you that you possess the abilities that are needed to master the specific goal, and that the success you envision is, in fact, attainable. The feedback has to be delivered in genuine fashion by someone whom you consider to be credible.

If you receive this kind of feedback, you are likely to mobilize greater effort and sustain it over a longer period of time compared to occasions when you do not receive this social persuasion. In other words, the positive statements give a boost to your sense of personal efficacy, and as a result, you try harder.

When there is an absence of positive feedback, you end up dwelling upon your imagined deficiencies or thoughts of self-doubt. This interferes with your goal-directed efforts. Worse yet, when you receive active criticism or are told that you lack the relevant capabilities, you tend to avoid goal-directed efforts altogether. You stay away from the challenges that would ultimately help you secure success.

Unfortunately, it is often easier to undermine self-efficacy beliefs through negative feedback than it is to strengthen self-efficacy beliefs through positive encouragement. That means it is crucial to become choosy about the people with whom you share your financial goals.

If you are striving to pay off debt, you should probably not share this goal with people who are likely to say "Well, you shouldn't have accumulated the debt in the first place," or "In today's economy, that's an unrealistic goal." Instead, try to surround yourself with friends and family members who are likely to say "It's definitely doable, and I know you have what it takes to do this."

Sometimes, as a bonus, we receive encouragement when we least expect it. A friend of mine is trying to pay off a loan at her credit union. She said she has been trying to make payments that are larger than the minimum required payment each month. After handing her check and payment coupon to the teller, the teller said, "Good for you for making larger payments. The amount of interest you will ultimately pay on this loan will drop. It will really make a big difference." I'm impressed by this credit union for supporting their members. And I'm impressed by this teller who seemed to know just what to say to give my friend a boost in her sense of personal efficacy.

Stress Management

As you've seen, when you make a judgment call about your capabilities and assess whether you have what it takes to reach a particular goal, you rely in part on information obtained from the outside (feedback, signs of progress, and so forth). But self-efficacy research suggests that you also rely on information acquired by conducting an *internal check*.

Most of the time, this check-in process is not deliberate, formal, or even fully conscious. It is a quick scan that you complete to gather data about your physiological state (level of tension, arousal, energy, and so forth) and your emotional state (mood and stress level). You then interpret this data and use it to determine whether you feel ready to take on your goal. You are more inclined to make a positive judgment of your capabilities (that is, strengthen your sense of self-efficacy) when you are not bothered by negative physical or emotional states.

For example, imagine that your goal is to become a savvier investor. Every Saturday, you read about investing, you review the performance of your own stocks and mutual funds, and you decide whether you should take any action to manage your accounts. If, while you are engaging in these tasks, you notice a knot in your stomach, muscle tension in your body, and overall feelings of anxiety, you may interpret this stress reaction as a sign of vulnerability to poor performance.

"Darn," you think to yourself, "I must not be cut out for this. I doubt I should even be experimenting with the stock market." The end result is a diminished sense of personal efficacy. The fears and self-doubts grow and eventually trigger additional stress and tension that actually help to create the inadequate performance you fear. Perhaps you choose to get out of the market altogether rather than tolerating the discomfort.

Alternatively, you may notice the physical and emotional arousal but decide that they are not bothersome states. Instead, you interpret the stress reaction as confirmation that you are taking on an exciting endeavor: "I am getting a charge of energy because I am taking on something new and challenging. No doubt, the extra energy will facilitate my efforts." Here, the results of your internal scan enhance your perceived self-efficacy. You charge forward, armed with a boost of confidence.

As you can see from this example, you can strengthen your self-efficacy by reducing your stress reactions and being careful not to misinterpret your physical and emotional states.

Now you have four different ways to boost your confidence that you have what it takes to modify a financial habit. All four methods are simple, accessible, and easy to arrange. Take an inventory of which components of self-efficacy are already working in your life and which components you can add. Then answer the following questions.

Reflection Questions

If a friend asked you to explain the concept of self-efficacy, how would you describe it to him or her? What example would you use from your own life to illustrate the concept?

Describe how you can use the four components of self-efficacy in the service of strengthening your confidence that you will reach your specific financial goal.

Chapter Seven:
Persistence

"Take a method and try it. If it fails, admit it frankly, and try another. But by all means, try something."

-Franklin D. Roosevelt

"...in the end, mastery often involves working and working and showing little improvement, perhaps with a few moments of flow pulling you along, then making a little progress, and then working and working on that new, slightly higher plateau again."

-Daniel Pink

Your change journey is now well underway. You are approaching your money goal with readiness, confidence, and an attitude of experimentation. Instead of letting setbacks get you down, you are learning from them so that your change plan evolves in a purposeful direction.

Despite your careful preparation, you may still find yourself lacking in persistence when you get to the middle of your change journey. It is easy to get bogged down by the barriers that spring up in your path. Imagine that your supply of energy and enthusiasm is bubbling forth from a well. The well tends to run dry somewhere in the middle of a change project. In order to persevere in pursuit of your goal, you have to find clever ways to replenish the well.

The scientific literature on *persistence* gives you strategies to meet this challenge. Persistence goes by many different names in the research literature. Angela Duckworth of the University of Pennsylvania calls it *grit* and describes it as perseverance and passion for long-term goals.[1] She writes, "Grit entails working strenuously toward challenges, maintaining effort and interest over years despite failure, adversity, and plateaus in progress."

Edward Deci and Richard Ryan of the University of Rochester speak about *self-determination*.[2] They claim that when people are self-determined, they are energized to sustain effort toward long-term goals that are interesting, engaging, and personally meaningful. Other researchers have examined variations on persistence such as habit, goal attainment, and resilience.

Whatever the name, be it grit, fortitude, tenacity, or stick-to-itiveness, the concept of persistence contains important elements that help you maintain your momentum when the going gets rough. Strategies that help you persist include: (1) creating a sense of urgency, (2) fostering resilience, and (3) following the rules of practice.

Create a Sense of Urgency

As I suggested in the first chapter, the central dilemma in the management of finances is a motivational dilemma: We *intend* to do certain things to take care of our money, but we can't seem to make ourselves actually *do* them.

The reasons for deficient motivation are plentiful. One reason is that the consequences to poor financial habits seem too far off in the future. If you don't catch a regular glimpse of the dismal financial future looming on your horizon, you don't feel compelled to change things in the present.

Another reason for deficient motivation is that in general, people are reluctant to work on problems that they don't easily recognize. If you can live your daily life avoiding all evidence of your money problems, you don't see the need to change your habits. And you can actually arrange these conditions. You can ensure that you don't see, feel, or recognize your bad habits by rationalizing your decisions, normalizing your behaviors, and becoming skilled in the use of excuses, lies, and half-truths.

Unfortunately, the overall culture supports short-sightedness and the use of excuses. We live in a culture of "instant gratification." The default setting is to allow the temptations of the present moment to overshadow any plans for the future. If you actually want to do the things that financial health and security require (making short-term sacrifices for long-term gain), you are forced to swim against the current.

The attitude that will sabotage your chance at a great financial future is that of complacency. If you are content with debt, satisfied with overspending, and unaware of the danger of excuses, you will not be motivated to change your money habits. The only remedy to this dilemma is to *increase your sense of urgency about your problem*. This means finding ways to keep the truth (the whole truth!) at the forefront of your consciousness.

One way to do this is to *ask yourself the difficult questions* that will unveil the complete story about your current financial situation, not just a partial story or a more convenient version. Here are three important questions that cannot be answered easily. They will require your time and brutal honesty:

- Which of my money habits are contributing to my overall financial problems?
- How controlled am I by my particular problem behavior?
- In what ways do I fail myself by not changing?

Another approach is to *visit your default future*.[3] This means taking the time to imagine the future that you will live if you continue your current unhealthy habits. You can take the exercise one step further by generating a list of the future consequences of your problem behavior:

How will my poor money habits affect my...

- self?
- family?
- retirement status?
- living conditions?
- participation in hobbies and interests?
- exposure to financial stress and worry?

Although it may sound counterintuitive, another strategy is to *increase the level of tension associated with your poor financial habits*. As a human being, when you encounter a truth that makes you feel uncomfortable, your natural tendency is to ignore it, suppress it, or push it to the back of your mind. However, discomfort can actually be motivating. If you find a way to hold the discomfort in a prominent place in your mind, you can use it in the service of change.

Try calling to mind your *moments of discomfort*. You know the ones—they are the moments that you are embarrassed to admit to yourself, let alone share with your friends and family members. Have you had to borrow money to cover your monthly bills? Has your credit card been rejected at a store? Do you get calls from debt collectors? Do you consider overdraft fees on your checking account and high interest payments on your credit card balance to be normal? Do you ever purchase a "want" when you can't even cover your needs? Do you spend more than you earn?

Now, as you focus on your moments of discomfort, notice what feelings arise. Do you notice fear, self-disappointment, or dread? Great! These feelings can create a sense of urgency and get you moving toward your goal before it's too late. Better to experience these emotions now when you still have the opportunity to change your behavior, rather than later when the emotions are compounded by regret.

When you notice yourself lagging in your change efforts and you need a boost to your persistence, pull out your moments of discomfort and allow yourself to feel the emotional consequences. You can also look for new ways to increase your sense of distress. For example, you may schedule that long-overdue talk with a financial counselor to review the current state of your money affairs. Or you may rent a documentary about debt in America. Another option is to talk with an individual who has had to maintain employment well into his golden years because he did not save enough money for retirement.

All of these ideas will ultimately help you persist toward your money goals by raising the sense of urgency about the problem. Now let's look at a second way to strengthen your persistence.

Foster Resilience

When psychological researchers study *resilience*, they study individuals who do "OK" or even "better than OK" after they have endured a traumatic event, some kind of adversity, or some kind of risk.[4] Famous examples of resilient individuals include Helen Keller, Anne Frank, and Christopher Reeve. In the financial domain, several individuals (who are now household names) claim to have overcome humble beginnings to become wealthy. Several others started out rich, proceeded to lose all of their money, and then built up a fortune again (think Dave Ramsey or Donald Trump).

Resilient individuals face an obstacle and *not only adapt, but achieve something greater than what they had before*. This impressive feat has led researchers to examine why such individuals are able to persist and achieve growth while others are simply crushed by dire circumstances. By studying resilient individuals, researchers have uncovered some of the factors that predict resilience when dealing with adversity. Two of the factors that predict resilience are a problem-solving orientation and positive emotion-inducing coping.[5-8]

What does it mean to have a *problem-solving orientation*? It means that when obstacles arise, the individual perceives the situation as a problem that can and should be solved. His default setting is to generate a list of potential solutions right away. He does not sink into a victim mentality, believing that he is a helpless soul who cannot regain a sense of control. Nor does he assume a passive stance, just watching and waiting for the situation to resolve itself on its own. He takes action, even if it is just cognitive action at first (like brainstorming, researching, and planning).

Imagine a company that is facing financial challenges and considering a complete overhaul of the benefit package it provides to its employees. Perhaps the company announces that workers can expect to make higher contributions to their health insurance premiums, to receive fewer vacation days, and to lose the opportunity for raises during each of the next five years. As you can imagine, news like this sends most workers into a frenzy. Those without a problem-solving orientation become passively resigned to their fate. Morale drops, and they wait for the managers, administration, or the executive board to "fix" the situation somehow.

Those who *do* have a problem-solving orientation react differently. They talk to their managers and offer ideas for how the administration can minimize the damage to company morale and benefit packages (knowing that their ideas *may or may not* be considered). They educate themselves about the anticipated consequences to their take-home pay and generate hypothetical scenarios for their household budget. They plan to meet the financial challenge head-on by having a number of backup plans available to compensate for their lost income.

In this way, the problem-solving workers retain a sense of control and self-efficacy in a very difficult environment. This allows them to persist toward their goals.

A second factor that predicts resilience and persistence is *positive emotion-inducing coping*. This is the ability to create positive emotions to bounce back from negative emotional experiences.[8] The concept includes the ability to find positive meaning in negative circumstances.

When you are working toward a goal and you face a setback, there are many coping strategies available to you that will distract you from frustration, discouragement, or hopelessness. But the ideal coping strategies do more than just distract you from distress. They enhance the positive aspects of your well-being, too. In other words, they go beyond simply "neutralizing" a situation and allow you to emerge psychologically stronger after a mistake or failure. By finding positive meaning and positive emotions in negative circumstances, you will emerge stronger and better able to persist toward your goals. (Think of Nietzsche's famous quote "That which does not kill us makes us stronger.")

Positive emotion-inducing coping doesn't have to happen in grand style such as the person who loses all of his money and then uses his determination and positive spirit to gain it all back again. It can happen in smaller ways, too. Consider the receptionist who learns that she and her coworkers will soon experience a cut in pay. She decides to lighten the atmosphere and cheer up her coworkers with laughter instead of succumbing to the downward-spiral of gossip in the office.

Or consider the man who realizes he has made mistakes involving the overuse of credit. While paying down his debt, he decides to become a mentor to others to help them avoid similar mistakes. We have a popular expression in our culture that summarizes this coping strategy well: When life gives you lemons, make lemonade.

Of course, there are times when you dig deep within yourself, but you still cannot find the strength to squeeze the juice out of the lemons. These are the times when you may have to "fake it 'til you make it" (remember the "acting as-if" approach that was introduced in chapter two?), buckle down, and allow your persistence to grow from practice.

Follow the Rules of Practice

Think of something that you practiced in your life, perhaps as a child. Did you practice a musical instrument or a sport? Now think back to your practice sessions. Did they sharpen your skills over time, or were some of the practice sessions just the mere repetition of the same mediocre performance over and over again? Doug Lemov and his colleagues, in their book *Practice Perfect*,[9] point out that not all practice is valuable. While carefully designed practice can revolutionize your skills and enhance your persistence, poorly designed practice can ingrain bad habits and cause you to lose enthusiasm for the activity.

Ensure that your practice helps you maintain effort toward your money goals over time by following a few simple rules.[9] Try to focus more on practicing the 20 percent of skills that will create the most value rather than the 80 percent of skills that do not make very much difference. When you make an error, go back and fix it as soon as possible—you want to achieve correction immediately after a mistake so that you do not inadvertently reinforce it.

For example, if you are trying to establish a Saturday morning routine of reviewing your budget and you realize one Sunday morning that you forgot to do it that weekend, sit down and do it on Sunday morning. Do not wait until the following Saturday, because you will reinforce the habit of putting it off.

Learn what essential skills you are lacking, and practice those. Identify people who are already achieving the very goals that you would like to achieve, and work to develop the same financial skills that they have. Once you have broken down your performance and mastered the practice of specific skills, try bringing those skills into the authentic context in which they will ultimately be used.

Are you settling in for some good, old-fashioned practice? Before you begin, you may wish to read the next chapter. Practice and persistence are powerful techniques, but they cannot stand alone. They must be accompanied by impulse control to help you withstand the temptations that threaten to derail your practice sessions. In chapter eight, you will learn ways to strengthen your discipline and sustain your goal-directed efforts.

Reflection Questions

Think of someone you know in your life whom you would consider persistent (or "gritty," as Angela Duckworth calls it[1]). What is it about that person that allows him or her to keep working on something challenging long after everyone else has given up?

When you think of your past financial behavior, what are your moments of discomfort? What feelings arise when you call to mind these memories of your past missteps? How can you use these feelings constructively to increase your sense of urgency for change?

What are the areas of your financial life in which you could benefit from using more of a problem-solving orientation?

Activity

Design a practice session in which you work on one of the isolated skills that will create the most value as you pursue your specific money goal.

Chapter Eight:
Impulse Control

"Grant us a brief delay; impulse in everything is but a worthless servant."

–Caecilius Statius

"I generally avoid temptation unless I can't resist it."

–Mae West

Let's face it. Sometimes you want your self-control to come from the outside because when you check out your internal supply, you see that the fuel gauge reads "empty." Enter the "Mother Bear" wallet designed by John Kestner, a graduate student at the Massachusetts Institute of Technology.[1]

Kestner realized that it is easy to lose touch with the visceral sensation of spending money when you pay for your purchases with credit cards, debit cards, or other non-currency means. Your credit cards fail to work when you surpass your credit line, but they do not give you any warning when you near the upper limit of the budget that you set for yourself.

The Mother Bear wallet is constructed with a hinge that becomes more difficult to open when you cross a preset threshold. You get to decide in advance (when you have an adequate supply of self-control) how much you feel comfortable spending in a given month. Then, you set the threshold on your wallet (via smart phone), and it gives you a tangible reminder of your budget by tightening the hinge as you get closer to your predetermined limit.

If the Mother Bear wallet isn't for you, consider another way to boost the supply of self-control that is available to you when you really need it. An interesting study in the Journal of Consumer

Research[2] suggested that you can tighten your muscles—in your hand, finger, calf, or biceps—as a way of strengthening your self-control. The investigators put study participants in a range of situations in which they had to withstand immediate pain in order to achieve a long-term gain. For example, in one experiment, participants had to consume an awful-tasting beverage that would, in the long run, benefit their health.

The authors found that when participants were instructed to clench their muscles while trying to exert self-control, they were better able to withstand pain and discomfort. However, the muscle tightening only worked when the assigned task was consistent with the participants' goals (for example, to have a healthier lifestyle). Also, the technique only worked when it was used at the moment their self-control was being tested. It did not work if they tightened their muscles in advance of the challenge.

It is unclear if the findings of the study will help people who are trying to reign in impulsive spending, but it seems that it is worth a try. Just imagine being in your favorite store, admiring an item that you have been longing for, and feeling tempted to reach for your wallet. Perhaps at that moment in time you clench your fist and recite a reminder to yourself in your head ("No! As much as I deserve this item, I deserve financial abundance even more!"). It might just interrupt the old sequence of *see-desire-spend* long enough for you to escape the store without opening your wallet.

What if self-tightening wallets and muscle-clenching aren't your thing? Thankfully, more conventional methods exist to strengthen your self-control, and I will present them in this chapter. First, though, I will discuss the importance of impulse control as well as the evidence that it is an exhaustible resource. Then, I will debunk the popular myth that you can control temptation by simply controlling your thoughts. After considering what does *not* work, I will present several strategies that *do* work, along with exercises and activities to help you apply them.

Importance of Self-Control

One of the greatest psychology experiments of all time gives us important clues about the importance of self-control. The original study was conducted by Walter Mischel at Stanford University in the 1960's.[3] The purpose of the study was to understand when the capacity for *deferred gratification* (the ability to wait in order to attain something that you want) develops in children.

In the experiment, Mischel brought four-, five-, and six-year old children into a room, one at a time, and sat them down in a chair. On the table in front of them was a marshmallow. Mischel explained to each child that he was going to leave the room for a few minutes. While he was away from the room, the child could decide to either (1) eat the marshmallow right away, or (2) wait until Mischel returned and then have two marshmallows. Then Mischel left the room for 15 minutes.

It turned out that many of the children could not delay gratification for the entire 15 minutes, and they ate the single marshmallow shortly after Mischel left the room. However, approximately one-third of the children were able to delay gratification long enough to receive the second marshmallow. The experiment confirmed the original hypothesis that the ability to override your impulses and patiently wait for a reward is determined by age.

Far more interesting than that initial finding is the conclusion reached by the follow-up studies that were conducted ten or more years later. Many of the original research participants happened to be friends of Mischel's three daughters. As the friends entered their teens, Mischel began to hear stories about their academic achievement and general life success. He began to suspect that there was a connection between certain aspects of their performance in their adolescent years and how they fared on the "marshmallow task" many years before. He began sending out questionnaires to all of the teachers, parents, and academic advisers of the original participants to ask them about the teens' coping competence, social competence, self-regulatory strategies, and academic performance.

Mischel managed to obtain follow-up measures for 185 research participants. When analyzing the measures, Mischel found dramatic results. Compared to the children who were able to delay gratification for the whole 15 minutes, the children who ate the marshmallow quickly had more behavior problems, had trouble managing stressful situations, had difficulty paying attention, found it harder to maintain friendships, and achieved S.A.T. scores that were a full 210 points lower than the other group.[4]

The moral of the story, then, is that the ability to wait, to delay gratification, and to control your impulses is an attribute that is important for success in multiple domains of life.

Of course, this lesson about self-control is significant for your money behavior. Think of all of the occasions when you might benefit from waiting: pausing before making a large purchase, gathering all of the data about an investment option before jumping in, and allowing the magic of compound interest to do its thing. Self-control is clearly an important asset in many financial scenarios. Individuals with a greater reserve of self-control will often have the edge over those who are more impulsive.

Indeed, there are studies that demonstrate a link between self-control and financial success. In one large-scale study,[5] researchers followed the lives of 1,037 individuals from New Zealand from the time they were 3 years old until they were 32 years old. When the participants were young, the researchers observed them and gathered information about their level of self-control from their teachers and parents. They continued to follow these children during adolescence and then again in adulthood to see how they were doing on a number of measures of personal, social, and financial success.

The results showed that childhood self-control was a good predictor of health, prosperity, and financial security in adulthood. A closer examination of the findings revealed that the participants who showed better self-control as children went on to demonstrate better financial planning and money management skills as adults.

There seems to be something very important about self-control that allows it to have a widespread and long-term impact on behavior. Mischel believes that the qualities that underlie effective self-control may be crucial ingredients in the task of expanding your intelligent social behavior, allowing you to cope, solve problems, and regulate yourself better.[3] Whatever the specific mechanism, it is clear that people benefit from investing in the specific component skills and processes necessary for effective impulse control.

Limits of Self-Control

Unfortunately, self-control is a limited, exhaustible resource. Picture a bucket, and imagine that the water in the bucket represents self-control. When you wake up in the morning after a restful night of sleep, the bucket is full. You feel abundant strength and energy to engage in the daily tasks that require you to monitor yourself closely, focus your attention, be careful with your behavior, inhibit your impulses, and persist in the face of emotional obstacles.

When your bucket is depleted, however, it becomes much harder to think creatively in the face of temptation. You do not feel like you have the energy to modify bad habits or inhibit your impulses.

Many different tasks use up the supply of water in the bucket of self-control. The water level sinks lower each time you resist temptation,[6] hold back distressing emotions,[7] suppress forbidden thoughts,[8] and try to make a choice from an overabundance of options.[9] Included in that list are many of the situations that you may encounter on a daily basis, such as resisting doughnuts, making sure you don't speed on the way home from work, and managing the impression that you make on other people.

To make matters worse, you may work in an occupation in which you are expected to either enhance, suppress, or fake your emotions in the name of effective workplace performance. For example, counselors may need to suppress emotional responses when listening to clients, while storekeepers or salespeople may need to display a smile and good humor when assisting a customer. An entire body of literature is dedicated to this issue of "emotional labor," which is the term given to the task of managing emotions in the service of work role demands.[9] Emotional labor slowly drains your supply of self-control.

What is the end result of all of this restraint, suppression, and self-supervision? According to the research literature, the end result is diminished physical and cognitive stamina. You end up with smaller quantities of flexibility and creativity along with an inability to persist in the face of failure.

The official name for this is *regulatory depletion*. It means that if you use up much of your supply of self-control on one task, you have limited self-control available to use on the next task. For example, if research participants work hard to suppress their thoughts or feelings during an initial task, they have less stamina available to them to control their bodies or minds on a subsequent undertaking, even if it is a completely different task that is perceived to be unrelated.[7]

Consider the implications for your efforts to reign in spending. Imagine that it is the holiday season, and you have relatives staying at your house. When Uncle Fred visits, you have to work very hard to regulate what you say and do, because it is easy to invoke the wrath of this particular uncle, and *no one* wants that to happen.

You work hard to avoid certain topics of conversation (religion, politics, and that turkey incident from the 1987 Thanksgiving gathering). You resist the impulse to eat too many holiday cookies, because you don't want to prompt Uncle Fred's "fat jokes" again. And despite the fact that you are feeling decidedly miserable in your own home, you laugh at all of Uncle Fred's stories and display good holiday cheer.

Throughout his visit, your supply of self-regulation is steadily dwindling. You decide that you need a break from your relatives and head to the mall. You walk into your favorite store, armed with your wallet--but depleted of your resources for self-control. The consequences, of course, are disastrous.

You need a decent supply of self-control for other financial goals, too, besides managing your spending. It works to your advantage to control your impulses when designing a budget or directing your investments. As many financial advisers profess, the best investment strategies involve time and patience. Instead of getting distracted and overreacting to the performance of an investment in the short-term, we are encouraged to give ourselves time to obtain meaningful results. It is truly the long term that counts. And to stay focused on the long term, you need a strategy that strengthens your impulse control.

<u>What Does Not Work</u>

Unfortunately, the most common strategy that people use to strengthen their impulse control has been proven ineffective. That strategy is called *thought suppression*. Whenever you try to stop thinking about something in order to avoid temptation, you are employing this strategy. If doughnuts are your weakness and you try not to think about doughnuts, you are engaging in thought suppression. If you feel jealous of a certain individual and try not to have thoughts of jealousy anymore, you are engaging in thought suppression. If you have a habit of beating yourself up for your perceived failure and try not to have self-deprecating thoughts anymore, you are betting on thought suppression to save your fragile ego.

In a now-classic study on thought suppression, Wegner, Schneider, Carter, and White demonstrated the futility of this strategy.[10] Participants were asked to continuously verbalize their thoughts for five minutes. An additional instruction was that they were to *try not to think of a white bear*, but they were to ring a bell in case they did. The experimenters found the typical participant not only rang the bell several times, but also inadvertently mentioned the white bear or even worked the white bear into his or her stories. This showed the experimenters that thought suppression is both counterproductive and unsustainable.

This finding was later explained by the ironic process theory[11] which states that our attempts to control the unwanted thoughts paradoxically contribute to their recurrence. In other words, if we are going to check to see if we are thinking the unwanted thought, we actually have to activate the thought ("Am I thinking about a doughnut?" "Am I beating myself up for that miserable failure I had last week?"). The ironic process theory was later supported by researchers who studied the electrical activity of the brain during a thought suppression task.[12]

It seems rather logical that if you want to rid your consciousness of certain thoughts, you should stop thinking about them. But the evidence suggests (and you have to admit, your experience confirms) that this simply does not work.

Consider the woman who says "I am not going to buy another pair of shoes until I have my personal loan paid off." She chooses thought suppression as a strategy when she instructs herself: "I am not even going to think about shoes." When she walks into the department store, she begins to monitor her consciousness: "Am I thinking about shoes? Nope. Am I thinking about shoes now? Nope."

Given that she just primed the concept of "shoes" in her consciousness, what section of the department store will jump out to her first (and therefore, test her impulse control)? Undoubtedly, there are impulse control strategies that are much more effective, and I will review these in the next section.

What Does Work

Impulse control is best thought of as a multifaceted task. While any one of the following strategies may be helpful, you strengthen your self-control incrementally with every strategy that you add. For each goal you have, you may piece together a different combination of strategies. Overall, you are trying to mix and match strategies to design a comprehensive self-control "package" that can fend off any temptations that arise.

Strategy One: Manage Stress

The first strategy for strengthening impulse control likely feels both obvious and familiar to you, and there is good science to back it up. It is the idea that if you keep your stress level down, it is easier to maintain self-control.

Many people will readily admit that when they feel overwhelmed, they try to escape the emotional distress by looking to immediate sources of pleasure or good feelings, such as alcohol, high-calorie foods, or expensive purchases. Impulse control fails in these situations, because stressed individuals prioritize emotion regulation over disciplined behavior.

For example, consider the person who takes the time at the beginning of the day to plan a healthy dinner for the evening.

Then, after a stressful day at work, she comes home and indulges in junk food instead of the meal that was originally planned. A similar thing happens in the money domain when stressed-out people make store purchases that exceed their budget, buy things impulsively off the Internet, or make questionable financial moves.

Tice, Bratslavsky, and Baumeister conducted an interesting series of experiments to explore why our self-control breaks down during times of emotional distress.[13] In one study, the investigators asked the participants to read a sad story, imagine themselves to be the main character in the story, and try to identify with the emotions elicited by the situation. They were asked to write a brief essay describing how the story made them feel.

Then, the participants were asked to join in a taste test that was portrayed as unrelated to the story task. They were asked to taste pretzels, chocolate chip cookies, and cheese crackers and to fill out a questionnaire rating each food. Participants in the experimental group were instructed that eating does not improve your mood or make you feel better. Participants in the control group did not receive this instruction, allowing them to maintain the common belief that food can be used for comfort or as an effective way to cheer up.

The investigators then measured how much food was consumed by each group. Sure enough, they found that the experimental group ate less than the control group. Their conclusion was that when people are upset, they sacrifice impulse control for short-term, immediate pleasures. In other words, *when you are stressed, your need to cheer yourself up trumps your need to self-regulate.* This means that if you want to strengthen your impulse control in the service of long-term goals, stress management needs to be a key component of the process.

Strategy Two: Manage Cognitive Overload

A related strategy is to manage the amount of "stuff" that you carry around in your brain. A Stanford marketing professor named Baba Shiv conducted an experiment to demonstrate the importance of de-cluttering our brains.[14] The study participants were divided into two groups. The first group was asked to remember a two-digit number, and the second group was asked to remember a seven-digit number.

Each participant was asked to walk down the hall. At the end of the hall, participants were presented with a choice of two snacks: a piece of chocolate cake, or a bowl of fruit salad. It turned out that the participants who were given seven numbers to remember were almost twice as likely to choose the chocolate cake than the students who were given two numbers to remember.

Shiv concluded that the extra numbers functioned as a "cognitive load," meaning that they took up valuable space in the brain. This meant that there was less space available in the brain for it to do the important work of resisting temptation. The brains of the people who had to remember five extra pieces of information were so overtaxed, they were unable to participate in self-regulation, and they gave in to the decadent dessert.

Think of your brain like the working memory of your computer. Sometimes you have so many programs running, the computer isn't able to do its processing with any efficiency. If you close some windows, the processing speed picks up again. What do you have cluttering up your brain? See if you can discard any of it or write it down somewhere in order to free up valuable space for the hard work of resisting temptation.

Strategy Three: Strengthen Your Distraction Skills

Remember the marshmallow study described earlier in this chapter? It turns out that the children who successfully resisted the single marshmallow while the experimenter left the room were onto something important. Walter Mischel figured out that these children knew how to use the "strategic allocation of attention."[3]

This meant that instead of becoming obsessed with the marshmallow, they were able to shift their attention to other things, such as singing songs from *Sesame Street*, playing hide-and-seek under the table, or pretending the marshmallow was a tiny stuffed animal. As we know from the research on thought suppression, the children were likely not able to stop thinking about the marshmallow entirely. However, they were able to devote enough of their attention to distracting activities to allow their craving for the sweet treat to fade into the background of their minds.

This strategy of distraction has been studied extensively in the context of coping with pain and distress. Numerous studies have proven that distraction helps you cope with these stressors. The more of your attention a distraction technique requires, the more effective it is.[15]

Picture what this would look like for you as you work toward a money goal. Perhaps you call a friend when you are walking through the part of the store where your impulse purchases are most likely to occur. Or, when something pops up on your Internet browser that you are tempted to buy, you make yourself recite the alphabet backwards while you click to another site.

Better yet, perhaps you fill your mind with thoughts about the less tempting aspects of the item you are coveting (for example, "That laptop may look sleek, but it actually has less memory than my current computer....") If you identify in advance a handful of distracting activities that are likely to draw you in and keep you sufficiently engaged, you will have more success with this technique.

Strategy Four: Practice Mindfulness

From the perspective of the *mindfulness* school of thought, distraction is not encouraged. Practitioners of mindfulness agree that if you try to push a thought, feeling, or memory to the back of your mind, it intrudes more persistently upon your consciousness (just as the studies of thought suppression have found). These practitioners instruct that instead of trying to distract yourself from your distressing or tempting thoughts, you should open your awareness to them and accept them. Indeed, this is what mindfulness is: *attentive awareness of the present moment and a calm acceptance of one's thoughts, feelings, and sensations.*

Acceptance has a paradoxical effect: If you give full permission for a thought or feeling to be present, you take the power out of it, and the thought or feeling can then fade to the background. Students of mindfulness are often taught *defusion* techniques which allow them to create distance between themselves and their distressing thoughts. They are also instructed in *experiential acceptance* techniques which help them expand their awareness to be large enough that their problematic feelings are only one small part of it.[16]

When it comes to coping with urges to spend impulsively or other temptations that threaten your financial status, what strategy is best: distraction or acceptance? Unfortunately, science does not seem to have a specific answer to that question yet, but there is a hint from a related body of research.

Investigators who study food cravings have compared the effectiveness of acceptance- versus control-based strategies.[17] At the beginning of the study, the participants received either no intervention, instruction in control-based coping strategies such as distraction and cognitive restructuring, or instruction in acceptance-based strategies. Then they were given transparent boxes of chocolates and were asked to carry them around, but not eat them, for 48 hours.

Results suggested that the participants who rated themselves as *highly susceptible* to the presence of food in the environment were better able to exercise self-control using acceptance-based strategies. However, participants who rated themselves as *low in sensitivity* to the food environment and who used acceptance strategies experienced greater cravings.

The results are preliminary but suggest that different people benefit from different impulse control strategies depending upon their psychological makeup. This is probably the case for financial behavior, as well. We will need many more well-designed research studies before we can confidently match an impulse control strategy to each unique individual.

Strategy Five: Train Your Discipline Muscle

We know that people vary in their ability to choose successfully between conflicting desires and impulses. We also know that the road to success often requires self-discipline, or choosing long-term gain over short-term pleasure.

Research on self-discipline has shown that it is a crucial factor in predicting people's future success. It forecasts who will be able to do what is required of them (and therefore achieve important goals) versus who will wander down the path of whatever pops into their head. For example, studies have shown that students' level of self-discipline is a better predictor of their future academic success than their scores on intelligence tests.[18]

There is fascinating evidence that self-discipline can be "taught" or strengthened in children through games such as *Touch Your Toes*. This simple game requires children to touch their heads when the leader says "Touch your toes," and to touch their toes when the leader says "Touch your head."[19,20]

The adult version of self-discipline is called "grit."[21] It's a concept I mentioned briefly in the last chapter, because it's a way of thinking about persistence. The concept has an impulse control component to it, as well. According to Angela Duckworth, if a person is "gritty," he or she is not thrown off course by disappointment, failure, adversity, boredom, or plateaus in progress. While an impulsive person might use these elements as an excuse to give up, the gritty individual chooses to keep working strenuously toward challenges.

Studies of discipline in adults have revealed that self-control is like a muscle that can be built up with practice. If you ask people to add one small self-control task to their lives and to practice it regularly (for example, improve your posture, refrain from swearing, brush your teeth with your nondominant hand), they actually increase their overall supply of self-discipline.[22] Amazingly, even the most trivial of self-control practice tasks has the power to improve people's self-control for the challenges that they care about the most.

It seems that building up your self-control muscle allows you to be a better self-observer and to pause before acting impulsively. When faced with a choice between immediate pleasure and long-term benefit, a strong self-control muscle will allow you to pass over temptation and to choose the more difficult path.

Imagine how this skill might benefit you in your financial life. If you strengthen your self-control muscle, it will be so much easier for you to save part of your paycheck instead of spending it all, to be patient with long-term investments instead of reacting to bumps in the road, and to pay off debt instead of being lured in by the more immediate pleasures that your money can procure.

Your new skills in self-control will then generalize to other areas of your life. For example, Oaten and Cheng[23] have shown that a group of people who were trained in better money management not only gained better control of their spending habits, but they also became more disciplined in other areas: They became better at regulating their eating, alcohol intake, emotions, and household chores. That's not a bad outcome for the price of a regular self-control workout!

Psychologist Kelly McGonigal offers three categories of willpower workouts that are effective.[22] First, you can decline to do something that you regularly do, like using a particular habit of speech or crossing your legs when you sit. Second, you can add a new habit to your life, such as calling someone regularly or meditating for five minutes a day. Third, you can count something that you don't usually track, such as how many hours of TV you watch or how many flights of stairs you climb in a day.

These small exercises will help you build up your supply of "grit" or discipline, increasing the chances that you can use it in the areas of your life that matter most.

Strategy Six: Pause and Plan

You know the scenario: You are driving to work and looking forward to your first cup of coffee when suddenly, the car next to you veers into your lane. You take quick evasive action and then notice signs of the "fight-or-flight" response in your body. After the rush of adrenaline, your heart is pounding, your hands are shaking, and it takes a few minutes to regain your composure.

The fight-or-flight response is familiar to most people as the biological signature of stress. It's a useful response to have when you need to react quickly to a threat and keep yourself out of harm's way. It's *not* very useful, though, when you need to slow down and think through a tempting situation, like whether you should spend money in your favorite online store. Not only will the fight-or-flight response fail to help you in this case, it will actually sabotage your capacity for careful decision-making. That's because the response inhibits the part of the brain that is in charge of impulse control.

What you need in this circumstance is a biological response pattern that *enhances* the capacity for flexible, thoughtful action. Thankfully, such a response pattern exists. Psychologist Suzanne Segerstrom has named it the "pause-and-plan" response.[24] Unlike the fight-or-flight response, this response actually puts your body into a calmer state. Even more importantly, it gives more time and energy to the parts of the brain that are responsible for impulse control. This makes you better able to resist temptation, ignore distractions, and delay gratification. This is precisely what you need when you are tempted to spend money impulsively.

Interesting research has emerged that suggests you can actually trigger the pause-and-plan response by shifting to slow, deep, even breathing.[25] If you can slow your breathing rate down to four to six breaths per minute, you can shift your mind and body out of "stress mode" and into "self-control mode." The slow breathing triggers changes in the brain and body that help you to think flexibly and creatively and to solve the problem at hand. Said simply, breathing slowly helps you access your impulse control. Next time you want to do something but know that you shouldn't (like making that impulse purchase on eBay), or when you know you *should* do something but really don't want to (like cut up your credit cards), try spending a few moments slowing down the breath.

Strategy Seven: Consider Your Timing

Earlier in the chapter, I used the metaphor of water in a bucket to explain that self-control is a limited, exhaustible resource. When the bucket is full, you feel abundant strength and energy to monitor your financial behavior, focus your attention, inhibit your impulses, and persist in the face of emotional hurdles. When the bucket is depleted, these tasks become much more challenging. The level of the water in the self-control bucket sinks lower each time you have to hold back distressing emotions, suppress your thoughts or opinions, manage the impression you are making on others, or resist temptation. The timing of your financial decisions, then, is crucial.

For instance, if you have already drained your supply of self-control for the day, that is probably not the best time to be shopping, designing a budget, or making decisions about your savings and investments. Browsing your favorite store when your supply of self-control is low is just as dangerous as grocery shopping when you are hungry!

Think of it this way: Label the water level in your bucket of self-control as "0" when the bucket is empty and "10" when it is full. Then, check on the bucket periodically throughout the day to monitor the water level and to notice any patterns. For example, when you come home from work, the water level might be a "3," but when you come home from vacation, it might be a "9."

A basic rule of thumb is to be certain that you are not participating in any significant financial transactions when the level of water is less than 7 or 8. If the water level is lower than 7 or 8, give yourself a mandatory "cooling-off period" before you act. Delay the transaction or the decision until the water level has risen again and you have the resources to think in a calm and flexible way.

Now you have some facts about the limits of impulse control and the strategies that will help you strengthen your supply. Coupled with the ideas from the previous chapter, these strategies will carry you far in managing the obstacles that have sabotaged your financial change efforts in the past. Spend some time examining the role of impulse control in your life. The reflection questions and activity may help.

Section Summary

In section two, you have learned about some of the most powerful change technologies that social science has to offer. You are now equipped to move well beyond the simple idea of "willpower," having several effective change tools at your service.

Of course, change does not occur in a vacuum. It occurs in the context of your thoughts, emotions, environment, and relationships. If you make individual change efforts without taking the larger context into consideration, your efforts may get eclipsed. In section three, you will learn how to align your environment, social relationships, and psyche with your change goals. This will help tip the scales of habit modification in your favor.

Reflection Questions

In general, how disciplined of a person are you? Would your friends describe you as someone who exhibits great impulse control across many domains, or would you be like the child who devours the marshmallow as soon as the experimenter leaves the room?

More specifically, how disciplined are you in the area of personal finance? Thinking back on your financial behavior over the past several months, are there particular areas where you could benefit from exercising greater self-control? What are those areas?

What are the specific elements of your day and your life situation that tend to drain your supply of self-control? For instance, do you have a job that requires you to monitor the impression you are making on other people? Do you have to resist the snack table every day at the office? Do you have to fight through traffic without losing your cool?

What changes can you make within yourself to make it more likely that you will participate in goal-consistent behavior? Do you need to reduce stress, reduce cognitive overload, or develop a practice such as mindfulness or deep breathing? When, where, and how will you do this? Be specific.

Activity

Set your watch, timer, or computer to sound an alert every hour on the hour for three days. When you hear the alert, check the level of water in your self-control bucket, label it on a scale of 0-10, and record the number on a piece of paper. After three days of recordings, notice if there are any patterns. For instance, does your level of self-control routinely dip just after you get home from work? Is there a time of day when your self-control tends to run high? When you notice patterns, decide what this means for the timing of your financial decision-making.

Section III

Chapter Nine:

Using the Environment in Your Favor

"The block of granite which was an obstacle in the pathway of the weak becomes a stepping-stone in the pathway of the strong."

-Thomas Carlyle

Temptation. It's all around you. You are immersed in an environment that encourages you to part from your hard-earned money.

You are embedded in your environment as a fish is embedded in water. If you could ask a fish to describe the impact that water has had on his life, he'd have trouble answering the question because he has never lived a day of his life without it.

In the same way, you've never lived a day of your life without the influence of the environment around you. Some days, the financial messages are blatant, like when you are walking through the mall on Black Friday and you are bombarded by reminders of huge sales. Other days, the influence is more subtle, like when you encounter the impulse items in the checkout lane at the grocery store.

Because you are embedded in your environment, each situation that you enter has more power to control your habits than you think. As much as we like to believe that we are in full conscious control of our choices, legions of studies have shown that is simply not true.[1] Our goals can be reinforced or sabotaged by the world around us without our knowledge. We are especially vulnerable to these forces when we are stressed, distracted, or short on time.

It is important, then, for you to increase your awareness of the ways the environment is controlling your habits. Once you can spot the ways your context is helping you and hurting you, you can work out a plan to use the environment in your favor.

<u>Conduct an Environmental Inventory</u>

Perhaps the simplest place to start is to take a good look around and notice which environmental cues are working for and against you. Factors that may work in your favor include visual reminders of your goals. Have you put charts, graphs, or pictures of what you are aiming for around the house? Have you put your goal in writing and posted it on the bulletin board? Do you have inspirational messages about your new identity written on post-it notes and sprinkled strategically around your workspace (remember this from chapter two?).

Factors that may sabotage you include advertisements in newspapers, in magazines, and on television, as well as the sales fliers that come in the daily mail. Other things that can undermine your best efforts include easily accessible credit cards, easily accessible stores, bookmarked links to your favorite shopping websites on your computer, and so on.

Now see what you can change in your environment that will reduce temptation or fortify your persistence. You want to *increase access to positive cues and increase distance from negative cues*. The strategy is commonly used in realm of personal health. When you want to lose weight, you get rid of all of the high-calorie, high-fat, or sugary foods in your pantry. You get rid of the candy dish on your desk at work. You begin associating with like-minded people who also believe in the importance of maintaining a healthy weight. In place of the menu from the local pizza delivery establishment, you hang on your refrigerator door a photo of how you wish to appear. You do whatever you can to create an environment that supports healthy choices.

Now imagine transferring this strategy to the financial domain. How would it work? Perhaps you replace the romance novel on your nightstand with a copy of Kiplinger's Personal Finance magazine. You limit your access to credit cards by cutting them all up except one. (The remaining credit card gets frozen into a block of ice to eliminate the possibility of impulsive use!) You put pictures that remind you of your financial goal in strategic places around the house. You set your computer's screen-saver to read "abundance" or "security" or whatever financial concept you value. You redesign your route home from work to make sure you avoid passing by your favorite store.

Think about the elements in your environment that have tripped you up in the past, and get rid of them. Then think about the elements in your environment that have given you inspiration and support in the past, and add more of them.

Make the Right Habit Automatic

In one of my favorite books about change, *Switch: How to Change Things When Change Is Hard*, the authors stress the importance of making the right behavior easier and the wrong behavior harder.[2] One of the best ways to make the right behavior easier is to take the willpower struggle out of it completely and to set it as your default.

Studies have shown that human beings have something called a *default bias* or a *status quo bias*. This basically means that once we have things arranged in our lives, we tend to remain on the path of least resistance and stay with the default option.[3] Many times, people don't even bother to rearrange things when they know that an alternative arrangement would serve them better. For instance, most people who invest in a retirement savings plan choose an initial asset allocation and then leave it, never returning to rebalance their portfolio.[4]

The default bias can work in your favor when you set up automatic occurrences of your desired behavior and then leave them in place. For instance, want to save more? Set things up so that a certain percentage of your paycheck is automatically deposited into your savings account, your Roth IRA, or your 401(k) account. Want to avoid the late fees on your student loan payment? Set it up so that the payment is automatically deducted from your savings account each month.

Want to avoid paying interest on a credit card balance? Call the credit card company and ask them to lower your credit limit to a specified amount that you know you can pay off completely each month (yes, you can do that!). That way, you will never be able to build a balance that you cannot pay off in full each month.

Here's another example: In the book *Nudge: Improving Decisions About Health, Wealth, and Happiness*, co-author Richard Thaler describes a retirement plan that he designed called "Save More Tomorrow."[4] When you sign up for the plan, you agree to place all or part of your *next* salary increase into your 401(k). In this way, you are committing to automatically saving money that you have never gotten used to spending in the first place. When the salary increase occurs, the new default setting kicks in, and participants don't even miss their money.

Use Tools

Think back to elementary school when they taught you that one of the hallmark features that distinguishes modern man from his prehistoric ancestors is his ability to use tools.

As it turns out, one of the key features that distinguishes the financially savvy from the not-so-savvy is the ability to use tools. Thankfully, you don't have to keep financial records by chiseling them into a rock anymore. Many creative and inspirational digital tools exist to help you monitor a money habit. I'll list some of the websites that support behavior change in general, followed by a sampling of websites that support financial change.

Websites that Support Behavior Change

www.stickk.com: This website guides you through the steps of building a "commitment contract" that basically signs you up to achieve a specified personal goal within a particular time frame. The site offers you the option of putting money on the line to raise the stakes and apply gentle self-pressure. If you achieve your goal, you give a predetermined amount of money to "a charity, an anti-charity, or even that neighbor who keeps stealing your newspaper." You select a referee who monitors your progress toward your stated goal. And you enlist supporters who cheer you on as you pursue your change journey.

www.habitforge.com: Here's an accountability website that lets you sign up to start a new healthy habit, then sends you daily emails to see how you did the day before with regard to your goal.

You can either "go solo" or "join a group" to undertake this venture. You can go the "21-day" route, which asks you to engage in your new healthy habit for 21 days in a row—if you miss a day, the count starts over. Alternatively, you can choose a "thumbs up" or "thumbs down" option to provide feedback on your progress.

www.43things.com: This site describes itself as the world's largest goal-setting community. Here, you make a list of your goals and share them with others. You document your success, share progress, and ultimately use the support of the community to help you make progress on the 43 (or fewer) things that matter most to you.

www.getupp.com: Getupp calls itself a "location-based commitment service." If you are motivated by public humiliation, this might be the right website for you. Getupp is a Facebook-based app that allows you to specify what you are going to do, when you need to do it, and how flexible the due date is. Then, you choose if you want to alert all of your friends about your success or failure each time you have the opportunity to work toward your goal.

www.quantifiedself.com: Quantified Self describes itself as "a place for people interested in self-tracking to gather, share knowledge and experiences, and discover resources." The website hosts a blog, a forum, meetups, and conferences, among other things. If you are passionate about gathering self-knowledge through numbers, you may thoroughly enjoy this site.

www.changeanything.com: This website has been developed by the authors of the book *Change Anything: The New Science of Personal Success*. It has a blog, video clips, and other content that supports the task of creating an effective personal change plan. Some of the website content is reserved exclusively for people who have purchased the book. The book gives readers a code to access a free limited-time premium subscription.

Websites for Tracking Financial Change

mint.com

buxfer.com

readyforzero.com

learnvest.com

budgetpulse.com

Note that this is not, by any means, an exhaustive list. New websites and apps are designed all of the time. The key is to find one that fits well with your environment and life situation.

<u>Design Rules</u>

Earlier I mentioned that Chip and Dan Heath, authors of *Switch*, suggest that you should do whatever you can to take the willpower struggle out of the equation and make the right behaviors easier. You can do this by creating rules for yourself. With a well-written rule, you specify exactly which healthy action you would like to see yourself pursue in situations that put you at high risk for blind repetition of unhealthy habits (remember implementation intentions from chapter three?).

If I want to make an unplanned purchase that costs more than $25, then I will go home and think about it for two days before making a decision.

If I feel defeated when I look at my net worth spreadsheet, I will compare it to my net worth from one year ago and appreciate the progress I have made.

If I experience jealousy and longing when I see my neighbors drive by in their new car, I will make a list of five great things I have done with my money since I have finished making car payments.

If you have a large amount of debt that needs to be paid off soon, you will need to put fairly strict rules into place, at least until your situation becomes more stable. Here are several examples:

I will pay for all of my purchases with cash.

I will block access to my favorite online shopping sites.

When I go to a store, I will always bring along a trusted friend or family member who is aware of my current money goals.

I will not bring any money with me to work (use this one if you find yourself splurging for fancy coffee beverages or getting suckered into buying things for your coworkers' kids' fundraising projects).

If I need cash, I will make myself walk to an ATM (use this one if the ATM is a good distance away from your present location!).

I will attend meetings with a financial educator once per month and be open about the current state of my finances.

Create Action Triggers

A common behavioral technique that prompts you to do things that are not yet a part of your regular routine is called an *action trigger*. This is the act of pairing a new behavior with an object or an action that is already an automatic part of your day. In this way, you don't need to battle with temptation or fight with competing urges to ensure that you engage in goal-consistent behavior.

The basic formula for an action trigger is: *When X happens, Y happens, too*. This is the easiest way to establish a new habit, because it ensures that you will execute a certain desirable action that you have specified in advance. Consider these examples:

When I turn on my computer, I will check my account balances.

When I turn the calendar page to a new month, I will update my net worth spreadsheet.

When I change the clocks for daylight saving time, I will rebalance the funds in my 401(k) or 403(b).

Linking a new behavior to an established one advances the new behavior from an effortful and voluntary process to an automatic, natural, programmed action. This is a good way to protect a new habit from excuses such as "It's OK to make an exception this time" or "I'll start tomorrow."

How can you pair goal-consistent habits with actions that are already a part of your everyday routine?

Once you have started using rules, tools, objects, and actions to prompt the money behavior you wish to see, you are well on your way to using the environment in your favor. Still, there is one very important part of the environment that we haven't looked at yet: people. Every day you are surrounded by people who can either help or hinder your goal-directed efforts. In chapter ten, you will learn how to arrange your social context to support your money goals.

Reflection Questions

Look around the room where you are currently sitting. What visual cues do you see in your environment that may serve as a positive reminder of your money goals? What do you see that may sabotage your financial change efforts?

Is there any way you can arrange for the automatic occurrence of a desired financial habit? What automatic processes are already working in your favor?

What tools and rules do you use as a method of keeping your money habits on track?

How can you design an action trigger that will routinely prompt you to engage in a healthy habit that will support your financial goal?

Activity

Take a ten-minute walk through a mall, shopping district, or commercial area of town. Count how many environmental cues you can find that prompt you to spend money. Notice some of the outrageous language that is used to create a sense of urgency for spending (think "doorbuster" or "blowout sale"). Notice some of the more subtle cues, as well.

Chapter Ten:
Change in a Social Context

"Choose your friends wisely—they will make or break you."

-J. Willard Marriott

"A tough lesson in life that one has to learn is that not everybody wishes you well."

-Dan Rather

"Be careful the environment you choose for it will shape you; be careful the friends you choose for you will become like them."

-W. Clement Stone

———————————

In chapter nine, you learned how to rearrange the environment to support your money goals. Inanimate objects like finance magazines, motivational pictures, and digital tracking systems can all be placed strategically around your living space to optimize your motivation. But people are a part of your environment, as well, and people cannot be moved and manipulated as easily as objects!

In this chapter, we will consider the somewhat tricky issue of arranging your social context to support your financial change efforts. You will start by identifying the people who are the cheerleaders in your life. Then you will identify the people who are blatantly sabotaging your money goals. Finally, you will determine who is subtly interfering with your efforts, and you will learn how to ask these people for specific help with your change project.

In this chapter, recognition goes to Kerry Patterson and his colleagues who, in their book[1], make the distinction between friends (who keep you on the road to health and happiness) and accomplices (who do not). I am grateful for the clarity they brought to this topic.

Cheerleaders

Cheerleaders are the people in your life who are on your side, no matter what. They are your biggest supporters on the road to change. Patterson writes, "These are the individuals who—actively and sometimes almost imperceptibly—help keep us on the path to success by modeling good choices, speaking up, holding us accountable, offering advice, and cheering us on."

Author Joyce Landorf Heatherley referred to these individuals as *balcony people*.[2] She uses a metaphor comparing life to a giant glass sphere. The bottom of the sphere is filled with dark, murky water. In the water reside the people (*basement people*) who are negative and critical toward you and who try to drag you down. They say hurtful things to you and try to get in the way of your efforts to be the best that you can be.

The top of the sphere is filled with clean, fresh air. This is where the balcony people reside. They are the people who believe in you, encourage you, and affirm your efforts. They want you to achieve your dreams and to be more successful. They do whatever they can to build you up and to infuse your life with confidence. Because they want you to be the best person that you are called to be, they give you a vision of doing something more with your life.

The balcony people are successful themselves. They have worked hard to create their own success, so they are not threatened by your efforts and are free to provide genuine encouragement. As far as they are concerned, there is plenty of room in the fresh air for everyone. Your job is to recognize these people and to spend as much time as you can with them. It is also your job to make sure that *you* are residing in the balcony, sharing hope and encouragement with the people whom you encounter.

The cheerleaders or balcony people in your life provide support in two fundamental ways: instrumental support and emotional support. When your friends or family members provide direct, concrete assistance by giving you goods, services, information, advice, or guidance, they are giving you *instrumental support*.

Here are several examples:

Uncle Fred gives you $100 to jump-start your rainy day fund.

Your neighbor, who is a financial educator, directs you to a free, local consumer credit counseling service.

After hearing a story about creative budgeting on the television news, your friend relays it to you.

A coworker recommends that you check out the flex-spending plan offered by your employer.

When the people in your life offer concern, caring, empathy, or encouragement, they are giving you *emotional support*. This type of support lets you know that other people value you, believe in you, and want you to succeed:

Your coworker says, "I'm sorry to hear you didn't get the promotion. I know you've been working hard on increasing your income and your retirement savings. I will cross my fingers for you that another position comes up."

Your financial educator says, "I know that you can reach your new savings goal, because I've seen you do amazing things in the past."

Of course, it is fairly easy to spot a cheerleader, because it feels good to be around them. When you sense that someone genuinely cares about the money goals that you set for yourself, you are in the presence of a cheerleader. It is in your best interest to try to increase the number of cheerleaders you have in your life and the amount of time you spend in their presence.

Improve the chances that you will find more cheerleaders by looking in the right places. Attend local seminars on money management and personal finance to meet other people who have goals that are similar to your own. Talk with coworkers who are at the same developmental stage as you, and find the ones who are upbeat, open, and enthusiastic about building their financial standing. Find a financial educator or adviser who feels like a positive, supportive person, and ask for the kind of reinforcement you need.

Saboteurs

On the complete opposite end of the spectrum from the cheerleaders are the *saboteurs*, or the people who actively sabotage your progress toward your money goals. Saboteurs are not necessarily engaged in outright fraud, like a corrupt adviser who funnels your life savings into a Ponzi scheme. They simply do something that actively interferes with your goals. For example, the spouse who takes money that is earmarked for an emergency fund and spends it on a new big-screen TV is acting as a saboteur. So is the roommate who is consistently late with his share of the rent, and the friend who intentionally chooses a pricey restaurant for your social outing when she knows that you are trying to pay down your debt.

Why do people purposefully try to stand in your way when they see you on the journey toward financial health? There are many possible explanations for this behavior, but here are four of the main reasons:

- *Fear of changing roles.* If you have always played a particular role in a relationship and your new financial standing may help you shift roles (for example, from "dependent wife" to "equal contributor to the household income," or from "individual who needs a roommate in order to keep the apartment" to "individual who can afford to live alone"), this may feel threatening to the saboteur. The relationship may only feel comfortable to him or her if you maintain your old role. Saboteurs will do anything, then, to pull you back into your old role if they see evidence of a transformation.

- *Feelings of discomfort.* When saboteurs observe you changing your money habits, you may be inadvertently holding a mirror up to their own behavior. This forces them to recognize that they have bad habits of their own that could use their attention. Rather than expend the energy to start a change journey themselves, the saboteurs will try to minimize their discomfort by reeling in your change efforts.

- *Feelings of inadequacy.* Many saboteurs simply do not feel good about themselves in general. It helps them feel better if they can "level the playing field" and keep you down somehow.

- *Comfort in the familiar.* Sometimes people try to pull you back into your old habits because it feels more safe and secure to stick with what is known rather than allowing you to risk a new habit that may or may not work out. Extreme examples of this include the people who tell you not to use debit cards, electronic banking, or ATM's, directing you instead to use cash and good old-fashioned transactions with a human bank teller. They have made a judgment call that there is safety in the status quo, and it is not worth putting that at risk.

After you have identified the saboteurs in your life, you need to decide what to do to manage them. The first general rule of managing saboteurs is to distance yourself from them, if at all possible. This could mean breaking off particular relationships or limiting the amount of time you spend with certain people. Of course, if the saboteur is a partner or family member, distancing yourself is probably not the best option.

Instead, you may try clarifying your goals and intentions and asking for the specific type of support that you need (I'll discuss "transformation conversations" a bit later in this chapter). Be open and specific about what you are working on, and give examples of the high-risk or tempting situations you are trying to avoid. If it is relevant, tell the saboteur how you think your new healthy habits will benefit him or her, too.

Unfortunately, even if you are honest and open about your money goals, there is no guarantee that the saboteur will agree to support them. Your next move might be to create boundaries around your goals, protecting them from the interference of others:

You move your emergency funds into an account that is solely in your name—no one else in your household has access to these funds.

You set a rule that if your roommate is late with his share of the rent more than two times in the next twelve months, you will ask him to leave and replace him with a more responsible roommate.

You give your friend the names of three or four restaurants where the two of you can meet and where the price is friendly to your budget. You tell her that you cannot meet with her unless it is at one of these establishments.

When Boundary-Setting is Difficult

Sometimes you know you need to set boundaries with a particular individual in your life, but you have trouble doing it because you are worried about the other person's well-being. Here is an example:

Sherri knew from the caller ID that this was a phone call that she did not want to answer. It was Katlyn again, her niece, likely calling to ask for more money. Katlyn is 24 years old, single, unemployed, and the mother of three children. The money she receives from the state's welfare program is barely enough on which to survive, and so she has come to rely upon her aunt's generous monetary gifts as supplemental income. The problem is, Sherri cannot really afford it. She is less than ten years away from retirement and has not been able to make any contributions to her employer-sponsored retirement fund, because of all of her spare cash goes to Katlyn.

When the phone starts ringing, Sherri is resolute that she will not give in this time to help Katlyn escape her latest financial dilemma. However, with each successive ring, she feels the knot of guilt in her stomach begin to grow. She thinks, "The last time I refused to help Katlyn, she got so annoyed with me. I just can't tolerate her being angry and upset. Besides, it's not only Katlyn who needs help; her three little children need me. Someone needs to step in." With that thought, she answered the phone, prepared to do whatever she needed to do to help.

Sherri has a generous heart. Thank goodness there are people in this world who have such a generous spirit and who want to help those in need. As you can see from the story, though, there are dangers associated with the habit of giving money away to others

124

rather than tending to your own financial goals. An individual like Sherri is in the habit of putting others first. She will spend money on others in order to keep harmony in relationships, only to realize later that money does not necessarily create healthy or rewarding interpersonal connections. In fact, she is actually enabling the dependency and helplessness of other people. Also, she is getting distracted from her own financial goals.

The word "enabling" grew out of the literature on addictions. It is now applied to any situation in which an individual chooses an approach that is intended to help another person, but ultimately, the approach perpetuates problematic behavior. Sherri provides a great example of this. Of course, she intends to help Katlyn and is in fact helping her on a temporary basis. But in the long run, the practical effect of Sherri's "help" is that Katlyn does not learn to become financially responsible and independent. Katlyn is shielded enough from the pain and hardship of her poor financial situation that she does not feel the drive or the motivation to change her own situation or to learn a better way. Sherri had nothing but good intentions, but she ended up perpetuating the problem.

Enabling behavior does not do anyone any favors. It essentially prevents others from learning valuable skills that will make them more responsible and resourceful. Also, if you are spending your time trying to protect someone else from the negative consequences of their choices and behavior, you have less time (and perhaps less money, as in Sherri's case) available to pursue your own financial goals. It is easy to get drawn in to another person's situation so deeply that you rarely resurface to evaluate your own.

One potential remedy here is to learn the difference between compassion and enabling. You can act in a compassionate way toward other people without perpetuating poor habits. When you are enabling other people, you have jumped into their situation with both of your feet. It is easy, then, to become lost in their reality and worldview. When you act with compassion, however, you leave one foot grounded in your own situation and worldview, and you place your other foot in the other person's perspective. This allows you to be empathic about the other person's dilemma, but it also allows you to remain reality-based and to retain an objective, problem-solving stance. You will be a much more effective helper when you are acting with compassion rather than enabling.

Another potential remedy is to strengthen your assertiveness skills. If you have trouble saying "no," consider saying, "I need some time to think about your request; I will get back to you." Then talk it over with a trusted friend who has strong boundaries. If you really want to help, consider whether there is a creative way to provide assistance that will not enable the help-seeker and will not derail you from the pursuit of your own money goals.

Find a meaningful way to be valued as a whole person rather than being valued for your financial contributions. Do you feel you have to give your money away to other people in order to earn their acceptance, love, companionship, or approval? It is a common belief, but one that will wreak havoc on your personal finances. Do some soul-searching to discover what personal worth and value you have that is not dependent upon your money. If this is really difficult, ask a friend for help. Or if this is too personal of an issue, sort it out with a psychologist or counselor or spiritual adviser. Discover new ways to make a contribution to other people's lives through non-material means.

Accomplices

So far it has been fairly clear. Cheerleaders are the people who stand on your side when it comes to your financial goals; saboteurs are the people who stand in your way.

Kerry Patterson and his colleagues name a third category of people who influence your habits: *accomplices*. Like saboteurs, accomplices prompt you to behave in ways that run counter to the healthy goals that you have set. However, accomplices do not actively interfere; rather, they exert bad influence in subtle ways. As Patterson describes it, "...many of your accomplices do nothing more than cast a shadow that affects your choices."[1]

One way that accomplices do this is by changing your view of what is "normal," reasonable, and acceptable. When the people around you struggle with the same bad habits that you battle, they change your sense of the overall norm. Their skewed vision may somehow make the unacceptable seem acceptable: "What, you only have $70,000 worth of student loans? That's nothing! I have $80,000." Or, "Who has money to contribute to a retirement fund? We use every penny of our paychecks." Or, "The only people who don't have mountains of debt are the rich people, and I wouldn't want to be one of them."

Another way that accomplices exert negative influence is by standing by and remaining silent when they see you getting yourself into financial trouble. It's the man who watches his friend take out a huge loan for a small business idea that he knows is doomed to fail. It's the couple who smiles and nods when their friends (who have exorbitant debt) share their philosophy of buying a new car every three years to ensure that they never have car trouble. It's the woman who knows that she and her partner should be saving for their retirement, but she is afraid to bring up the topic. The silent accomplices know what is unhealthy about a given situation, but they do not feel comfortable enough to speak up and share their wisdom.

Patterson discusses a category of accomplices that he calls "hosts." They are the individuals who enjoy sharing your weaknesses and who facilitate your bad habits by hosting events or get-togethers that prompt you to make poor choices. These events might include expensive outings, vacations, lunches, meetings, or recreational activities. If you are spending money you do not have to associate with certain people, these people may be "hosting" your bad habits.

If you hope to take control of your financial situation, you will need to take control of the social events that undermine your efforts. As Patterson suggests, "Scan for events and hosts that make your changes more difficult. Then either take charge of the event or take leave of it."[1]

Because accomplices exert a more subtle influence in your life than saboteurs, it will take thoughtful observation and reflection on your part to identify them. Take an inventory of the people in your life. If they are not cheerleaders or saboteurs, might they be accomplices? What level of importance do they attach to financial health? What do they want from you—your unwavering determination to reach your money goals, or your collusion with the bad habits they have established?

Once you have identified the accomplices, you do not necessarily have to kick them out of your life. You do, however, have to be vigilant of their influence and decide how to handle it. Perhaps you decide to propose alternative social events, meeting spots, or topics of conversation. Maybe you make a commitment to speak up in a calm, assertive, and tactful manner when you hear them trying to normalize poor financial choices. Or perhaps you give them permission to break their silence when they see you digging yourself into a deeper financial hole.

Transformation Conversations

Patterson suggests that there is great potential for transforming your accomplices into cheerleaders (or what he calls "coaches" and "fans") by holding a *transformation conversation*.[1] This is an honest talk in which you are very clear and specific about the support you need from the people in your life.

In a transformation conversation, you describe to another person the impact that his or her behavior has had on your efforts to change a habit. Then, you ask for the exact type of help you need. A transformation conversation should be carried out in a calm, non-accusatory way. Your aim is not to judge or blame the other person. It is to share your genuine thoughts and feelings about your problem and to ask for help in solving that problem. If you worry that you will approach the conversation in a way that will make the other person defensive, consider using one of these formats:

- I think (Here are the facts of the situation.)

- I feel (Here is the impact that the situation has on me.)

- I want (I am extending an invitation to engage in problem-solving with me.)

Example:

When we go to an expensive restaurant, I end up breaking my budget for the month, and I don't get to make my planned contribution toward paying down my debt. I am starting to feel hopeless that my financial situation will never improve. Would it be OK with you if I choose the restaurant for our next three outings? (Or, the stronger version: *I will need to choose the restaurant for our next several outings, or else I will not be able to attend.*)

- Compliment (I am approaching you about this matter because I know I can trust you/I know you are a supportive person/and so forth.)

- Project (Here is what I am working on.)

- Request (Here is how you can be helpful to me.)

Example:

We've been working together for a while now, and I've really appreciated that we can talk about our money goals. I am trying to make sure that with each raise we get, I add a little bit more to my retirement contributions. Will you ask me about this each year to make sure I am doing this?

I know you want to be supportive of me, so I feel like I can approach you about this issue. When we are out shopping together and you see me spending more money than I should, it is probably hard for you to speak up because you want to respect my choices. But I am working on limiting my impulse spending, and I could really use help. If you see me spending more than $50 on a shopping trip, feel free to encourage me to rethink my purchases.

Think of yourself as "coaching" others in exactly how they can assist you. Be as specific as possible about what actions you would like to see or what words you would like to hear. Many friends will jump at the chance to provide extra support. Many accomplices will feel relieved that they now have permission to speak up instead of standing by and remaining silent when they see you engaging in financially questionable behavior.

Know that some of your accomplices may refuse to help. They may be so invested in their own bad habits that it is too threatening to entertain the notion of change, even if it is *your* change rather than *their own*. Or they may feel scared that if they help you, it will threaten the future of your friendship. If accomplices are unwilling to help, see what you can do to respect their decision and then distance yourself from the specific behavior that enables your bad habits.

Some people believe that extra assistance or support "doesn't count" if it does not come spontaneously from the other person. In other words, if the help has to be prompted by a transformation conversation, it is somehow less desirable. In that case, ask yourself which is better for you—prompted support, or no support at all?

No matter what the outcome, it may be worth it to try to have at least a couple of transformation conversations. The ultimate benefit may be the awareness you gain about who is on your side and who is not. You are embedded in your relationships, so it is worth it to know the influence that these connections have on your financial goals.

Patterson points out that social support can be one of your most powerful change tools, because it has a dual effect: "Every time you transform an accomplice into a friend, you win twice. You remove the influence of someone who is pulling against you while adding someone who is pulling for you." That's not a bad payoff for a small investment of your time and energy.

Reflection Questions

Who are the cheerleaders in your life? How can you increase the number of cheerleaders you have in your life and the amount of time you spend in their presence?

Who are the saboteurs in your life? What do you need to do to manage them or distance yourself from them?

Who are the accomplices in your life? What are the ways in which they "cast a shadow that affects your choices?" Which of the accomplices would be willing participants in a transformation conversation?

Activity

Plan the next transformation conversation that you need to hold. Map it out using the "I think/I feel/I want" format. Then map it out using the "compliment/project/request" format. Which format feels more authentic and natural to you? What is the specific request that you need to make?

Chapter Eleven:
Taming Self-Sabotaging Thoughts

"The greatest discovery of our generation is that human beings can alter their lives by altering their attitudes of mind. As you think, so shall you be."

-William James

"Carefully watch your thoughts, for they become your words. Manage and watch your words, for they will become your actions. Consider and judge your actions, for they have become your habits. Acknowledge and watch your habits, for they shall become your values. Understand and embrace your values, for they become your destiny."

-Mahatma Gandhi

Just as you are surrounded by your environment and your social relationships every day, you are also embedded in your thoughts and beliefs. They are another important part of the "context" in which your money habits play out. Your thoughts can have a profound influence on your financial choices in a positive or a negative direction.

Are your thoughts on your side, or are they sabotaging your money habits? Put your thoughts to the test with help from the following quiz:

Read the following list of statements. If you agree with a statement, check off the item.

- o I'm way too busy to be able to focus on my finances.
- o If I am successful in changing a money habit, I won't be able to keep the changes going.

- o I nod in agreement when my financial educator or financial adviser makes suggestions for improving my budget or my savings strategies, but he doesn't really know what's right for me.

- o It takes so much energy to just take care of the day-to-day stuff (work, household chores, parenting), there is no energy left to devote to personal finances.

- o Working on my finances would just add another layer of stress to my life.

- o I've resigned myself to being "poor," because that's easier than making changes to my saving and spending habits.

- o I consider it to be my partner's job to take care of our finances. It's not my job.

- o My efforts to improve my financial standing always end in failure, so it's not worth it to try anymore.

How did you do? Did you check off any of the boxes? Don't feel bad if you did. These are really common thoughts and beliefs that interfere with people's best efforts to change their behavior.

The good news is that you can learn to tame self-sabotaging thoughts. You can learn to catch them when they appear, to challenge them, and to replace them with more helpful thoughts. Let's start with one particular category of thoughts that is often problematic.

Permission-Giving Thoughts

One category of thoughts that interferes with your change efforts is called *permission-giving thoughts*, also known as *facilitating thoughts*. These are the thoughts that make your bad habits seem reasonable. They are the excuses that set you up for failure because they allow undesirable behavior to continue unchecked.

For example, consider a woman who is tempted to stray outside of her monthly budget. Here is a list of potential permission-giving thoughts:

It's not really a violation of my budget because it is extra money that fell into my hands.

I've had a busy day at work and I'm entitled to some extra pampering.

I'll do it just this one time, and then I'll get back on track.

If I do it just this one time, I won't need to do it ever again.

I'll stray just a little outside of my budget, and that won't hurt anything.

Everyone else can spend whatever money they want, so I can too.

I deserve to treat myself.

Can you see how these thoughts give the green light for the wrong behavior? If you make a list of the excuses for why your bank balance and your net worth don't look the way you prefer, you'll find that many of the excuses fit this pattern.

If you find yourself using several permission-giving thoughts, know that you are not alone. Human beings are masters of the art of excuses. There is an entire line of scientific inquiry dedicated to this issue. It is called "behavioral economics," and it explores the cognitive biases that interfere with your thinking as you make important financial decisions. It is firmly rooted in the cognitive and social psychology research that examines why people make seemingly irrational decisions when it comes to money.

Once you have identified a facilitating thought, your next step is to question it with the objectivity of a scientist or a detective. Ask yourself the following questions:

- If I keep using this permission-giving thought, will it take me closer to my ultimate financial goals or farther away from them?

- Am I ever secretive about this thought? Why do I hide it from other people? How would my behavior change if I had to be open and honest about this thought with everyone I know?

- What would my life look like if, for all intents and purposes, this thought ceased to exist and there was no possible way for me to use this excuse?

- What is the payoff I am getting when I use this facilitating thought? Is it allowing me to avoid something? Is it protecting me from something? Is it giving me an "easy way out?" Is there a way for me to be courageous and forgo the payoff?

Now you have a sense of how this thought is operating in your life. By examining the thought in an objective fashion, you have gained a healthy distance from it. You are no longer caught in the hold of this thought. Instead, you have the power and the flexibility to tear the thought apart—and then keep the part that is working and discard the part that is not.

At this point, you may consider writing a "rational response" to your thought.

Examples:

Facilitating thought: *I deserve to treat myself.*

Rational response: *I do deserve to treat myself, but I have a problem sticking to my budget and getting my bills paid. So it is healthier for me to treat myself with the free activities that I love. Once I am engaged in a fun activity, I won't even be thinking about my temptation to spend money I don't have.*

Facilitating thought: *I'll splurge just this one time.*

Rational response: *If there were no possible way for me to use this excuse, I'd have to deal with the discomfort of passing up a tempting purchase. It would be on my mind for a while, but the discomfort would eventually come to an end. I might even get to the point where I feel a sense of pride and accomplishment that I am better aligned with my money goals.*

Distressing Thoughts

There is a second category of thoughts that interferes with your best laid financial plans. Call them distressing, depressing, gloomy, or pessimistic, these are the thoughts that paint a negative view of the possibility for change.

Psychologist Aaron Beck listened carefully to the statements made by distressed people and realized that the statements reflected three main themes: negative thoughts about the self, negative thoughts about the world or environment, and negative thoughts about the future. He called this the *cognitive triad* and advocated a system of identifying, challenging, and replacing these thoughts.[1]

Examples:

Self

I am a failure at managing money.

I am worthless when it comes to understanding financial concepts.

World

Some people are rich and some people are poor; the world is just unfair that way.

Everyone is out to take my money.

Future

I'll never be in a place where I'm satisfied with my finances.

There's no hope for a decent retirement.

How do you catch your gloomy thoughts? Next time you notice yourself experiencing a negative emotion in connection with your finances (like frustration, disappointment, or defeat), try to identify what you were thinking just before you started feeling bad. Look for any thoughts that seem to have a broad or sweeping negative quality to them, such as "I'm *always* worthless," or "The world is *never* fair."

Another good exercise is to think through the three categories of the cognitive triad and to conduct a self-inventory. Ask yourself if you ever: (1) make critical or self-disparaging comments about your ability to manage your finances; (2) assume you are at the mercy of an unfair world that is determined to drain your wallet; or (3) predict that the future will be no better than the present.

A third way to catch your distressing thoughts is to search for any *negative feedback loops* that occur regularly in your life. A negative feedback loop is a series of events that begins with a distressing thought and ends with a worsening of the distressing thought, sending you spiraling downward into helplessness and hopelessness. At times, if you have a sense that a negative feedback loop is occurring, you can trace it to identify the thought or belief that keeps the whole loop in motion. The loop usually follows this pattern:

Distressing thought → Negative emotion → Diminished energy, focus, and motivation → Inability to take action toward your goal (or, engaging in behavior that actively sabotages your goal) → Belief that you cannot get back on track → Reinforcement and worsening of the original distressing thought.

Consider the real-life example of Jan (not her real name). Jan noticed that she started each month with the best of intentions. She designed a reasonable budget that allowed her to pay all of her bills, make a reasonable contribution to her retirement account, and save money for the future purchase of some of her "wants." She even built flexibility into her budget to account for unanticipated expenses.

Still, despite her planning, she found that she couldn't keep herself within budget. Each month, her outcomes were farther and farther away from her target. Jan felt her finances spiraling out of control. She sensed that a negative feedback loop might be the culprit.

Investigating the situation further, she discovered that there were only two or three unplanned purchases each month that broke her budget. The purchases occurred when she feeling tired and out of sorts. She felt tired and out of sorts when she was experiencing guilt. And she felt guilty when she thought of herself as a failure in the area of personal finances. In other words, the loop looked like this:

"I'm a failure when it comes to managing my money." → Feelings of guilt → Diminished energy, focus, and motivation → Making an impulse purchase that is not within the budget → Additional guilt and the belief that she will never get back on track –> Confirmation that she is a "failure" when it comes to managing money.

Now that Jan has identified the distressing thought, "I am a failure when it comes to managing my money," she will need to challenge and replace this thought with a more balanced and helpful thought.

In this way, she will interrupt the negative feedback loop. She will begin to work *with* her thoughts rather than fight against them.

Challenging and Replacing Distressing Thoughts

Many times when you are thinking thoughts that lead to guilt, frustration, discouragement, or hopelessness, it is because you are making certain *thinking errors* in your mind. Thinking errors are distortions in your reasoning that twist the truth, making things seem worse than they really are. Here are several examples of thinking errors that commonly occur in the context of personal finance:

All-or-nothing thinking (You cannot see the middle ground; everything is either black or white):

- *Either I will adhere to my budget plan perfectly, or I won't follow it at all.*

- *I'm not able to make the whole payment on my electric bill, so I'm not going to pay anything this month.*

- *I didn't agree with all of the advice that my financial adviser gave me, so I'm going to ignore everything he said.*

Overgeneralization (You make assumptions about the future based on one or two events):

- *My efforts to improve my financial standing always end in failure, so it's not worth it to try anymore.*

- *Things always turn out worse when I attempt to fix them.*

Magnification (You zero in on one problem or mistake and then "make a mountain out of a molehill"):

- *The increase in my rent means that the cost of everything is increasing.*

- *The fact that I am tempted by impulse purchases means that I am fundamentally flawed as a human being.*

Should-statements (You set up a rule for yourself that is based on unrealistic expectations):

- *I should be able to afford the things that my neighbors can buy.*

- *I should be able to figure out my finances without help.*

Do you see how thinking errors skew your judgment and make it hard to appraise your situation realistically? If you truly believe your distorted thoughts, they can turn into a self-fulfilling prophecy. You start acting as if your predictions are true, and then your behavior produces outcomes that ultimately confirm your predictions.

Does it sound like a trap? It is. And it is a very common human phenomenon, too. People tend to react not only to the situations they are in, but also to the way they *perceive* the situations and to the meaning they assign to these perceptions. This means you have a powerful reason to take stock of your beliefs—especially the ones that create distress.

You may be wondering why you develop thinking errors in the first place. Sometimes we are powerfully influenced by societal messages, cultural beliefs, or stories in the media. Think about how many negative messages you have heard about the downturn in the economy that occurred over the last few years. You don't even have to be a regular viewer of the television news to be bombarded with stories of economic doom and gloom. The messages are everywhere. No wonder many people now hold the distorted thought: "The worsening economy means that there is no hope for people like me."

Another way we develop distorted thoughts is through previous life experiences. If you have lived through financial hard times, this may skew your perception of yourself and your world. Your experience of financial difficulties may have been long ago, when you were growing up. Or they may have been much more recent. Perhaps you have watched yourself accumulate debt over time, and your repeated attempts to pay it down have not been successful. Perhaps you were making ends meet, and then your life situation shifted and disrupted your financial balancing act.

In any case, when you live though a disappointing situation, your brain becomes hypervigilant, searching for any signs that the disappointment may recur. Your brain makes negative predictions to warn you about future hardship. However, the brain's warning signals end up being a double-edged sword: On the one hand, they serve a protective function. On the other hand, they prevent you from seeing your situation in an objective and accurate manner.

One final way that we develop distorted thoughts is through the actual or perceived messages we receive from others. As you learned in chapter ten, if you have the wrong people in your cheering section, you may become the target of criticism instead of support. If you hear critical messages too many times ("You won't measure up," or "You won't amount to anything," or "You won't fit in"), you may start to absorb these messages and make them a part of your sense of identity. Of course, this makes it hard to gain enough distance from the messages to realize that they are erroneous.

By now you may have some idea of the thinking errors to which you fall prey. If you need additional help identifying your thinking errors, try asking yourself the following questions:

- What goes through my mind when I think of myself having financial difficulties?

- What do I find myself thinking when my account balance is worse than expected, despite having followed my budget closely?

- What thoughts have led me to discontinue my efforts at saving my money in the past?

- What do I think when despite having followed my financial educator's/adviser's advice, my monetary situation does not improve?

- Do I have any concerns, worries, or fears that come to mind when I think about managing my money?

- Do I ever complain to other people about my finances/the economy? If so, what negative things do I say?

Once you've identified the main distorted thoughts that plague your consciousness, there are two things you can do to challenge and replace them. The simpler of the two methods is called the *two-column technique*. Find a piece of paper and draw a line down the middle of the page. In the left column, list your erroneous thoughts. In the right column, see if you can generate replacement thoughts or more balanced, alternative thoughts that help you think about the situation in a more reasonable, constructive way.

Examples:

Distorted and distressing thought:

The worsening economy means that there is no hope for people like me.

Replacement thoughts:

People in other countries of the world live in economic situations that are far worse than my own.

Dwelling on the downturn in the economy does not help me be any more enthusiastic about my personal financial goals.

I could be grateful that I have a stable job and the means to weather uncertain times.

I don't have to be happy about the economy, nor do I have to believe that it is fair. I can recognize the unfairness and still do what I need to do to optimize my financial situation.

Distorted and distressing thought:

My efforts to improve my financial standing always end in failure, so it's not worth it to try anymore.

Replacement thoughts:

I am overgeneralizing from a handful of disappointing situations. I need to remind myself that I can't really predict the future.

If I expect the negative to happen, I will create the negative. It's better to think of each attempt to improve my financial standing as a "fresh start."

Thank goodness that I have had the drive and determination to make a few attempts to improve my personal finances. Now let me use that energy and resilience again.

When you read through your list of replacement thoughts, you will find that some of them really resonate with you, while others seem to miss the mark. That's a normal occurrence. Look for the replacement thoughts that feel the most authentic to you, and work with those. See if you can repeat them to yourself several times and really absorb the meaning.

There is a second method you can use to challenge and replace your distorted thoughts. This method is a bit more time-consuming because it asks you to examine each thought and test it against objective evidence to determine how valid or accurate it is. The process is called *cognitive reframing* or *cognitive restructuring*. It involves asking yourself a series of questions to explore whether the thought is supported by the available evidence. If it is not (and many of our negative thoughts are not), you generate a more helpful alternative thought.

Here are the questions to ask yourself:

- What is actually true about this situation?
- What is the evidence that my thought is true and correct?
- What facts am I forgetting or ignoring?
- What errors am I making in my thinking?
- What are the true facts of the situation, and what am I making up or exaggerating?
- What are some other ways to think about this situation?
- If my best friend were having this thought, what would I say to support him or her?

- If my best friend knew that I was having this thought, what would he or she say to support me?

- Is there a more positive way to look at this situation?

- Is there any benefit I can find in this situation?

- What practical things can I do to deal with this situation?

- Is the situation really as bad as I am making it out to be?

- What is the worst thing that could happen?

- How likely is it that the worst thing will happen?

- If the worst thing happens, how would I handle it?

- What is probably, most likely, going to happen?

Example:

Original thought: *An overdrawn checking account again! I just can't get anything right.*

Alternative thought: *I am not proud of having an account that is overdrawn. But it is just a temporary situation, and I can fix it and view it as a learning opportunity. The worst thing that will happen is that I will have to pay some annoying penalty fees. It's not the end of the world. This does not define what I can or cannot do to manage my account in the future (in other words, I will watch out for the thinking error known as "overgeneralization"). A problem-solving approach is going to help me much more in this moment than guilt.*

When You Need Outside Help

Everyone thinks distorted thoughts occasionally. We are most vulnerable to distorted thinking when we are stressed, depressed, or tired. Typically, after our stress level returns to normal and we feel more like ourselves again, we are able to recognize our cognitive errors and correct them.

However, sometimes you need outside help to identify, challenge, and replace your negative thoughts and assumptions. If you are under prolonged stress or if you suffer from depression, you may have held your skewed beliefs for so long that they seem accurate and normal. When everything looks dark, you have no reason to question the negative thoughts that pop up in the darkness—they blend right in with all of your other thoughts.

In this case, it is worth it to listen to the feedback that you are getting from the people in your life whom you trust. Are they telling you that you are being overly negative about some aspect of your money management, your financial standing, or the economy? Do they encourage you to be more confident about your power to change your situation for the better while all you feel is "stuck?" Do they ever tell you that they are worried about your level of energy and motivation or your ability to focus?

If other people notice your negativity and at the same time, you are so immersed in it that you don't even see it anymore, you may need to seek outside help. Sometimes this means going directly to a mental health professional and asking for an evaluation. Other times it means going to a person who is trained to recognize emotional distress and who can refer you to the right place (for instance, primary care physicians and religious leaders are often trained to recognize depression and other stress disorders).

If you do suffer from depressive symptoms or another stress disorder, it is worth it to seek treatment as soon as possible. While your financial situation may have contributed to your depression in the first place, ongoing depression can have an adverse impact on your financial situation. This is because when you are depressed, you miss more work, become less productive at work, and put yourself at higher risk for job loss. You make poor money decisions and become more vulnerable to compulsive spending or binge spending.

Today, excellent treatments are available for depression and other stress disorders. One of the most popular interventions used in mental health settings is called cognitive behavior therapy (CBT). It is the approach that formed the basis for the ideas in this chapter. CBT teaches individuals how to identify, refute, and replace their automatic negative thoughts with more balanced thoughts.

Although the exercises in this chapter may be helpful to anyone, I cannot stress enough how important it is to **work with a qualified**

professional if your distorted thinking has risen to the level of a clinical diagnosis or if it interferes with your daily functioning and your sense of personal well-being. A financial educator or financial adviser will be able to help you down the road, but if clinical symptoms are present, your first visit should be to the office of someone who can properly assess your mental health needs.

The Power of Expectation

Earlier in the chapter you learned how distorted thoughts can lead to negative outcomes through a self-fulfilling prophecy. If you believe something negative to be true, it *becomes* true, because your actions and reactions are ultimately influenced by your beliefs.

Thankfully, you can use self-fulfilling prophecies in your favor, too, through the *power of expectation*. Researchers have repeatedly shown that when you expect something good to happen, your expectations can bend reality to some extent and bring the positive outcomes your way. The classic example of this is from the field of medicine: the placebo effect. If you are prescribed a sugar pill believing it is an effective pain reliever or antidepressant or sleep aid, your body responds appropriately and brings you the expected relief.

Researchers now know that the placebo effect extends far beyond the doctor's office. Author Chris Berdik reviews evidence of the placebo effect in multiple domains of life.[2] He describes a study in which people's expectations of the quality of wine they are about to drink actually changes the level of activity in the brain's reward centers. In another study, experienced weight lifters are told that they've taken a performance-enhancing medication, and then they are able to surpass their personal bests. In yet another study, track athletes are told that pre-race jitters actually heighten one's level of performance, and then their performance actually improves.

If you interpret a situation in such a way that it generates positive expectations of the future, you actually help to create good things in the future. Why not use this phenomenon to your advantage? What if you interpret a small positive change in your bank balance to be a sign of your resilience and money savvy? How about seeing your merit raise at work as a sign that you are destined for advancement? Use your thoughts to set yourself up for good things.

So far in this section, you have learned how to transform your environment, your social network, and your thoughts to guarantee that they support and protect your money goal. Now that you know how to modify your thoughts to ensure they do not function as an obstacle or barrier to your goal-directed efforts, it is time to turn your attention to your emotions. In chapter twelve, you will learn how to harness the power of your emotions in the service of your goal.

Reflection Questions

What are the facilitating thoughts that allow your undesirable behavior to go unchecked? What do you think your life would look like right now if these thoughts had never existed and there was no possible way for you to use these excuses?

What payoff have you been getting from using these facilitating thoughts? Is there a way for you to be courageous and forgo the payoff? Or can you arrange to get the payoff in a healthier way that does not hurt you financially?

What are the distressing thoughts and negative feedback loops to which you are most susceptible?

How have thinking errors skewed your judgment and made it difficult for you to appraise your situation accurately?

What are the "alternative" or "replacement" thoughts of which you need to remind yourself on a daily basis? What is a practical way for you to set up these daily reminders? Can you put them in crucial places in your environment, such as on post-it notes inside your wallet or inside your checkbook register?

How can you use the power of positive expectation in the service of your financial goal?

<u>Activity</u>

Conduct a real-life experiment to test the validity of one of your distorted and distressing thoughts. Follow these steps:

What is the thought that you will test? Rate the degree to which you believe this thought (0-100%):

What is an alternative thought, perhaps one that you do not believe as strongly? Rate the degree to which you believe the alternative thought (0-100%):

- What experiment could put your distressing thought to the test?

- What would you do?

- Where would it take place?

- When should it happen?

- What problems are likely? What are your plans to overcome them?

Now execute the experiment.

- What happened? What did you observe?

- What have you learned? How does this affect your original thought?

Re-rate the degree to which you believe your original thought (0-100%):

Re-rate the degree to which you believe your alternative thought (0-100%):

Chapter Twelve:
Harnessing the Power of Emotion

"Human behavior flows from three main sources: desire, emotion, and knowledge."

–Plato

"It is very important to understand that emotional intelligence is not the opposite of intelligence, it is not the triumph of heart over head—it is the unique intersection of both."

–David Caruso

As much as we would like to believe that our choices and our behavior are controlled by conscious verbal thinking, the truth is that our visceral reactions, emotions, and intuitions play a dominant role in causing our behavior. Any approach that promises to enhance motivation without addressing emotional factors will fall short.

Another way to say this is that you cannot make change happen and stick by simply modifying your thinking, or "putting your mind to it," as the expression goes. It seems you have to "put your emotions to it," as well.

This chapter begins by presenting evidence that emotions play a dominant role in your behavior. Then, you will learn three ways to think about the relationship between thoughts and emotions. Finally, you will read suggestions for how to harness the power of your emotions in the service of your money goals.

The Contribution of Emotion

Scientific studies have revealed that there are two processing systems at work in the mind as you move through your daily life: *controlled processes* and *automatic processes*. Controlled processes are the things that you think about consciously using language. Automatic processes happen without the need for conscious attention or control.

Whereas the controlled system might be viewed as an adviser to your behavior, the automatic system actually has more power to cause your behavior.[1] The automatic system includes your gut feelings, visceral reactions, emotions, and intuitions.

To get a better understanding of the influence of the automatic system, consider a 2005 study published by Brian Wansink.[2] In his experiment, he asked two groups of participants to eat soup. One group ate soup from regular bowls. The other group ate soup from bowls that were modified to be continuously refilled through a hole in the bottom of the table. Amazingly, the participants who were unknowingly eating soup from self-refilling bowls ate 73% more soup than the control group. However, when the researcher looked at the follow-up questionnaires that the participants filled out, that group did not even *suspect* they had consumed more.

What is the moral of the story? Much of your behavior operates underneath the radar of your conscious, controlled thinking. Multiple times each day, you carry out mindless and automatic behavior that is influenced by your emotions and intuitions. If you were questioned about this behavior, you would have no idea that hidden forces were driving many of your actions and decisions.

On the one hand, this is good because it gives your controlled processing a "break." It would get tiring if you had to deliberate about every mundane detail of your day, like taking a shower or driving to work. On the other hand, when your automatic system is running the show, you engage in mindless behavior. And mindlessness, combined with self-control problems, is the culprit for many bad habits.

Unfortunately, mindlessness runs rampant in our financial lives. Have you ever started the week with a couple of $20 bills in your wallet, only to find that they are gone by Wednesday and you can't remember where you spent the money? Are you fully aware of how much money you spend per month at the coffee shop, the workplace cafeteria, and your favorite fast-food restaurant? Or would you go into shock if someone did the math and showed you last month's totals?

Even if you make a determined effort to rely upon your controlled system to inform your choices and behavior, you are likely to underestimate the power of the automatic system. Consider the phenomenon known as the *hot-cold empathy gap*.[3] When you are in your calm, baseline ("cold") state of mind, you underestimate the impact that emotional arousal (or a "hot" state) will have on your behavior. You think that you will be able to behave yourself, set limits, and exert perfect self-control. You cannot fathom that your desires will be intensified and your decisions will be changed when you are under the influence of arousal. Then, you enter the actual situation, and all bets are off. Emotional arousal has a powerful pull on your behavior.

For example, when you are in a cold state and you imagine yourself walking into the bakery, you predict that you will simply purchase a black coffee—nothing fancy. After all, you know that you are on a strict budget this month because the car repairs need to be completed. You think through the situation rationally, and you *know* that this is what you will do.

An hour later when you walk into the bakery and smell the enticing aromas of flavored coffees and fresh pastries, you end up with a latte macchiato instead of a black coffee, and you spring for a box of cream-filled doughnuts to share with your coworkers. Despite your best intentions, you entered the "hot" state, or the non-thinking zone, and you broke the budget that you had set for yourself.

It is easy to see how mindless behavior and the presence of emotional arousal can sabotage even the best-laid plans. But even though emotions play such a dominant role in your decision making and behavior, it is possible to ensure that your thoughts and emotions work in harmony with each other to help you exercise self-control and reach your goals. Let's consider three ways to think about the relationship between thoughts and emotions.

Models of the Relationship Between Thoughts and Emotions

The first model is a fun one that was introduced by Jonathan Haidt[1] and then borrowed by Chip Heath and Dan Heath[4] for their book about organizational change. The authors describe a rider sitting on top of an elephant. The rider represents the rational part of yourself that is involved in logical thinking, advance planning, and giving you direction when you are working toward a goal. The elephant is the emotional, instinctive part of you that provides the energy and drive to keep you moving forward.

The rider and the elephant each have unique strengths and weaknesses. The rider's strength is conscious, controlled thought. He can see down the road and consult with other riders, thereby gathering valuable information that will help with the change efforts. He is good at planning, advising, and strategizing.

Unfortunately, the rider can get bogged down in overanalysis and overthinking, and he cannot order the elephant around against its will. Jonathan Haidt described the dilemma this way: "I'm holding the reins in my hands, and by pulling one way or the other I can tell the elephant to turn, to stop, or to go. I can direct things, but only when the elephant doesn't have desires of his own. When the elephant really wants to do something, I'm no match for him."[1]

The elephant's strength is getting things done. He has energy and drive because of his passion, gut feelings, visceral reactions, emotions, and intuitions. The elephant's weakness is that he wants the "quick payoff" and will stop in his tracks if he faces a long, treacherous road with no signs of progress or reassurance. He can be stubborn or lazy, and he is more interested in satisfying his immediate hungers and desires than hunkering down for a lengthy journey.

No progress is made when the rider and the elephant refuse to work together. As Chip and Dan Heath put it, "A reluctant Elephant and a wheel-spinning Rider can both ensure that nothing changes."[4] On the other hand, when the elephant and the rider collaborate, they "enable the unique brilliance of human beings"[1] and amazing feats are accomplished. When your thoughts and emotions are working together, you map out the best course to a new destination, and you use your emotions in the service of the journey.

Here is an example of what happens when the rider and the elephant are unable to get along:

You sit down at the beginning of the month, ready to design a no-nonsense budget that helps you surge toward your larger goals—like establishing a solid emergency fund, paying off credit card debt, and maximizing your contribution to your Roth IRA. You calculate how much money you will have after you pay your monthly bills, and you allocate the remainder to each of your goals. Later in the month, you feel frustrated, stressed out and deprived of fun because there is no money available for pleasurable activities. The feeling of deprivation builds and builds until you blow your budget—your friends invite you on a weekend trip to Vegas, and you jump at the opportunity.

Here is an example of better cooperation between the rider and the elephant:

Your monthly budgeting session begins with a thorough review of your needs (to pay the bills, establish a solid emergency fund, pay off debt, and contribute to your retirement account) and your wants (you know that pesky elephant wants to attend one fun event per week, and he wants to eat Chinese take-out once per month). You get a copy of the local newspaper and search the listings to find free or low-cost events to propose to your friends. After you pay your bills, you carve out a small "play account" specifically intended for the pursuit of fun and Chinese food this month. Then you allocate the remainder to each of your goals. Later in the month when your friends invite you on a weekend trip to Vegas, you find it easy to decline graciously.

The second metaphor is very similar to that of the rider and the elephant: it is the Planner and the Doer.[5] The Planner, using controlled processes and rational thought, peers down the road and decides what is best to promote your long-term well being and goal attainment. At the same time, the Doer, using automatic processes, stirs up feelings, desires, and all-around mischief. Just as the rider and the elephant are often at odds, the Planner and the Doer are often in conflict with one another.

A third way to think about the relationship between thoughts and emotions is the concept of *wise mind*, which comes from Marsha Linehan's system of psychotherapy called Dialectical Behavior Therapy.[6-7] Picture a circle that is labeled *reasonable mind*. An individual is in a state of reasonable mind when she uses logic, facts, and common sense to negotiate the world. She approaches reality through observable knowledge, numbers, equations, and cause and effect. Logic helps her to deal effectively with several aspects of reality. However, because many of life's problems have an emotional dimension, logic is not enough. She needs a second set of skills, as well.

Picture a second circle that overlaps the first one and is labeled *emotion mind*. An individual is in a state of emotion mind when he is reacting out of passion or strong feelings. His emotions become so extreme or intense that his logical thinking shuts down. Emotion mind helps him to experience love, devotion, desire, and persistence. However, if he stays in emotion mind too long, he may do things that are impulsive, irresponsible, or careless. Strong emotions distort his perception of a situation and magnify his excuses.

The area between reasonable mind and emotion mind, where the two circles intersect, is labeled *wise mind*. Here is where an individual integrates the logic of the reasonable mind with the sensitivity of the emotional mind to create balance.

Marsha Linehan compares wise mind to riding a bicycle. On a bicycle, you strive to stay upright by not leaning too far to one side or another. In life, you find wise mind by steering to find the balance between your emotions and your thinking. Although this takes effort at first, eventually you learn to jump on the bike and ride, making your skills more automatic through practice.

Think about the times when you have approached your personal finances by striking a balance between logic and passion. Chances are good that these are the times when you have been able to sustain healthy financial behavior for lengthy periods. Wise mind keeps you balanced so you do not fall into the trap of intellect (overly rational thinking that misses the emotional dimension of reality) or the trap of emotion (impulsivity).

Now you have three images that help you picture the ideal relationship between thoughts and emotions. The first is that of a rider sitting contentedly atop an elephant which is bumbling down a trail at a consistent rate of speed. The second is the image of a Planner (picture the most organized friend you know hugging her daily planner or her tablet!) shaking hands with a Doer (picture the most spontaneous and passionate person you know). The third is the image of two overlapping circles, with facts on one side, feelings on the other side, and wisdom in the middle.

A very important question remains. How do you arrive at this ideal relationship? How do you ensure that your emotions work with your thoughts and plans rather than sabotaging them? In the remainder of this chapter, I'll present general ideas for harnessing the power of emotions in the service of your goals.

Using Emotions in Your Favor

In most change situations, you can harness the power of emotions by (1) finding the feeling behind the need for change, (2) finding the optimal state known as *flow*, and (3) being careful about your *affective forecasting*. Let's consider each of these in turn.

When people ask you why you are working on a particular financial goal, it is easy to come up with an abstract, cerebral response such as "building security for the future" or "trying a new investment strategy." The reality is, to be motivated to work hard on a challenging goal over a long period of time, you have to be able to find the feeling behind your need for change. In other words, you have to be able to recognize the problem or solution in ways that influence your emotions, not just your thoughts. This means that you have to find something that hits you on an emotional level.

I recommend that you revisit one of the strategies that was introduced in chapter five: Take an honest look at what the future will be like if you do NOT succeed at personal change. The key question to ponder is "What will happen if you continue along your current path and you do not make progress toward your goal?"

This question may conjure up images such as the disappointment in your children's eyes when you tell them you cannot afford a trip to Disney World. Or an image of yourself desperately searching through the job ads after you retire from your main job and then realize you do not have enough money for your basic needs. Or an image of you receiving an eviction or foreclosure notice. Whatever the image, the key is to make it as rich and detailed as possible.

Alternatively, what hits you at an emotional level might be a picture of what the future will be like if you DO succeed at your financial goal. Here, you are creating images that give you a hopeful glimpse of the positive outcome of your hard work. You may picture yourself finally being able to give that special gift to someone who is important to you. Or imagine your child striding across the stage to receive his diploma at his college graduation, knowing that it was possible because of your financial contribution to his education. Or picture a specific scene of you enjoying your retirement rather than worrying about money.

How do you know if you need to create negative emotions (fear, anxiety, doom) or positive emotions (hope, joy, pride) in order to motivate yourself? After reviewing the literature, Chip Heath and Dan Heath[4] concluded that if you need quick and specific action toward your goal, it may be helpful to generate negative emotions. However, if you want to broaden your creativity, ingenuity, and flexibility in your approach to your goal, positive emotions will be most effective. In general, with long-range financial goals that are more ambiguous and require you to constantly refine your approach, you will benefit most from the open mind and broadened view brought forth by positive emotions.

You can also harness the power of emotion by finding the optimal state known as *flow*. Identified by Mihaly Csikszentmihalyi, flow is the mental state in which an individual is fully immersed in an activity with a feeling of energized focus.[8] A person who is in flow may be so absorbed in a task that he gets lost in his work. He may be described as "in the zone" or "in the moment."

A state of flow is often considered to be the ultimate goal when harnessing the emotions in the service of performance. In the state of flow, emotions are not just channeled or contained, but they are perfectly aligned with the task at hand.

Imagine an inverted "U." The area to the left of the peak represents the emotions that emerge when you are under-challenged. These emotions include boredom, listlessness, detachment, and annoyance. These emotions interfere with the performance of goal-directed activity. The area to the right of the peak represents the emotions that emerge when you take on a task that is too difficult. These emotions include anxiety and agitation, and they interfere with task performance, as well.

Flow is the peak of the inverted "U" where you have taken on a task that poses the ideal level of challenge. Your emotions are fully positive and congruent with your activity. As you execute the task, you feel a sense of connection with it. You are able to live in the present rather than regretting something from the past or worrying about something in the future.

To get into a state of flow, you need to accept a challenge that stretches you slightly beyond your current abilities, but not so far that you become uncomfortable or anxious. When the right balance is achieved, you will attain a degree of focus and absorption that allows you to be in the present moment and to work in harmony with your emotions. Imagine setting yourself up for a regular activity that will advance or reinforce your progress toward your goal and will allow you to operate in a state of flow. What would it be?

Examples:

Once a week, teach your kids or friends or neighbors about something interesting you have learned about personal finance (if they are willing listeners).

Turn your shopping outings (when you might be tempted by impulse purchases) into a game. Create a precise list of what you need, and see if you can guess what the total purchase price is going to be. When you get to the store, purchase only the items that are on your list, and see how accurate your guess was!

Another way to harness the power of emotions in the service of a change effort is to be cautious about *affective forecasting*. Research studies show that we make a lot of predictions about what the future will be like for us. Among other predictions, we make affective forecasts (or forecasts of our moods and emotions), attempting to envision what will make us happy in the future. Unfortunately, most of the time when we make such forecasts, we are incorrect.[9] For example, when research participants were asked to guess if they would be happier spending money on themselves or spending it on others, they incorrectly chose the former.[10]

To make this problem even more complicated, we tend to place disproportionate weight on the *beginning* of an experience when we are making an affective forecast.[11] For instance, when people make predictions about how much they will enjoy a physical fitness workout, they think about the initial phase of the workout, which is sometimes the most unpleasant. If participants are then prompted to consider *all* phases of the workout, their ratings of anticipated enjoyment increase.

You can probably relate to this in the financial domain. Have you ever dreaded balancing your checkbook, filling out the financial paperwork when you start a new job, or designing a household budget? You dreaded it because you were focused on the beginning of the task, which is likely to be the most arduous.

Did you notice that when you progressed a bit further with the task, other thoughts and feelings started to arise, and these thoughts and feelings were neutral or even slightly positive? Maybe you wouldn't go so far as to call it "enjoyment," but perhaps it was a feeling of pride or accomplishment. Perhaps it was a thought such as "Hey, this isn't so bad" or "I can do this."

The point is, if you can get over your "myopic focus on the initial unpleasantness"[11] and spread your attention over all phases of the task, it will increase your expected enjoyment of the task. This, in turn, may increase your intention to participate in the task. It's a classic example of assembling the right set of emotions to help you move forward rather than allowing emotions to keep you stuck.

Chapter twelve has shown you that your emotions can either be an ally or an obstacle in your change journey. Use the ideas from this chapter to draw upon the power of emotion to propel you toward your money goal. Spend some time thinking about how to supercharge your change efforts by not just putting your mind to it, but "putting your emotions to it" as well.

Section Summary

In section one, you prepared for financial change. In section two, you read about the behavioral techniques that are the driving force behind your change efforts. Now, in this section, you have added the framework that holds all of the pieces of change together. You have learned how to align your thoughts, emotions, environment, and social relationships with your change goals. In the final section, you will learn how to maintain your new, healthy behavior well into the future.

Reflection Questions

Can you think of a time when your best-laid financial plans were sabotaged by mindless, automatic behavior or by the surprise entrance of emotional arousal into the situation? How did emotions derail your efforts?

Which image of the relationship between thoughts and emotions appeals to you the most? The elephant and the rider, the Planner and the Doer, or the overlapping circles? Can you create your own image that is meaningful to you? How can you remind yourself of this image every once in a while?

What is the feeling behind your need to change? Create a rich image of what the future will be like when you DO reach your financial goal.

What regular activity can you set up that will advance your progress toward your goal and allow you to operate in a state of flow?

How can you disperse your attention across all of the phases of a financial task that you are dreading, making sure you are not getting bogged down by any initial unpleasantness that may occur at the beginning of the task?

Section IV

Chapter Thirteen:
Troubleshooting

"The measure of success is not whether you have a tough problem to deal with, but whether it is the same problem you had last year."

-John Foster Dulles

"You don't drown by falling in the water; you drown by staying there."

-Edwin Louis Cole

You now have many ideas about transforming your old habits into something new and arranging your life context to support financial health. You are beginning to put these ideas into practice.

The process of change can be long. Carol Dweck hit the mark when she described the process in this way: "…Change isn't like surgery. Even when you change, the old beliefs aren't just removed like a worn-out hip or knee and replaced with better ones. Instead, the new beliefs take their place alongside the old ones, and as they become stronger, they give you a different way to think, feel, and act."[1]

Your job is to continue using the techniques and strategies that work best for you. Use the reflection questions and activities at the end of each chapter to reinforce your learning. Through your participation in the exercises, you will discover new things (both good and bad) about yourself and your money situation.

When obstacles arise, you may be able to return to earlier chapters to gain assistance with self-efficacy, persistence, impulse control, or the stages of change. Alternatively, for extra help with troubleshooting, you may check out the ideas in this chapter. Here you will learn to distinguish between a lapse and a relapse. Then, you will discover how to get out of a difficult spot by learning the lessons of relapse, achieving greater perspective, and exercising self-compassion.

Lapse Versus Relapse

When you are working toward a money goal and you experience a setback, it is important to be honest with yourself and to evaluate whether the setback signals a lapse or a relapse. A *lapse* is a temporary detour off the path to change. For example, the day you fail to follow your budget after several days of disciplined behavior, you've had a lapse. It is a time-limited exception to your desired healthy habit.

A *relapse*, on the other hand, is an ongoing pattern of lapses. It's not just a temporary detour off the path to change; it's traveling down a different road altogether. For example, when you abandon your budget and you're not even trying to get back on track, you've had a relapse. The hopelessness and discouragement that accompany relapse may make it difficult for you to even imagine that you can resume goal-consistent actions.

The reason why it is important to distinguish between a lapse and a relapse is because they each require a different response. When you have a lapse, you can learn about the obstacle that diverted you off the path to change, shore up your resources, and return to your action plan.

When you have a relapse, however, you will need to reassess your stage of change (see chapter five), because you are likely revisiting an earlier stage. Once you determine your current stage of change, you will know which mental tasks will help you move forward again.

Perhaps the most challenging thing about relapse is the set of emotions that often comes with it: guilt, shame, embarrassment, frustration, and self-disappointment. If you're not careful, these emotions can get in your way. They will prevent you from coping actively with the obstacles that took you off the path to change.

If you feel any of these emotions weighing down your spirit, there are several things you can do. Let's examine them one at a time.

Learn the Lessons of Relapse

The authors of the stages of change model note: "After relapse, before committing to another round of action, most people benefit from a period of self-reevaluation in which they learn from their recent mistakes."[2] They suggest that there are several important lessons that can be gleaned from relapse.

Some of the lessons have been covered in this book. For instance, you have already learned that few people manage to overcome their problem behavior the first time around. It often takes several attempts to change a habit before making the new behavior stick. This means that relapse is the rule rather than the exception.

You have already learned that change is a winding road rather than a straight path to your destination. Change requires an attitude of experimentation and systematic efforts (not random trial and error) to assemble the personal resources and life conditions that you need to succeed. Change requires you to use the right processes at the right time to keep moving forward.

A new lesson to consider is that people often underestimate how much it will cost them (in time, energy, and emotional resources) to change a habit. They forget that you cannot reverse a deeply embedded pattern in a short time. They also forget how frequently they will need to exercise their new skills to counter the temptations that bombard them.

The positive side of this is that it is *common and normal* to feel surprised by the demands of change. Many people have felt overwhelmed by the enormity of the task, and yet they have gone on to become successful changers by using skills and strategies like the ones presented in this book. If you have learned to use mindfulness, thought challenging, and implementation intentions in previous chapters, you can now use these techniques to address the doubts and the distress that accompany the transformation of your money habits.

James Prochaska reminds us that there is potential strength in relapse: "The strength of relapsers is that they usually are willing to risk taking action again in the near future; their initial action gives them strength and courage."[2] In other words, when you relapse, you can think of yourself as a seasoned learner rather than a nervous neophyte. You are aware of the possibility of complications and have prepared yourself to face them directly as you recycle your change efforts.

Another lesson is that if you relapsed, you probably didn't do it by making a major, catastrophic mistake. Instead, you probably did it by making a series of *mini-decisions* that added up to have negative consequences.[2] For example, maybe you started spending more time with friends or acquaintances who have unhealthy spending habits. Or, perhaps you felt that your savings regimen was going so well, you could ease up a bit. According to Prochaska, these mini-decisions can lead you to shift your course away from the maintenance stage and toward relapse.

The encouraging take-away message here is that it will not take a major overhaul of all of your habits to get back on track. Instead, it will take a few strategic mini-decisions in the right direction and consistent practice of these corrective efforts to get back to your goal of permanent change. You can do it one mini-step at a time. When you get discouraged, remember this famous quotation from Jimmy Dean: "I can't change the direction of the wind, but I can adjust my sails to always reach my destination."

A final lesson is that distress is the most common cause of relapse. Emotional problems, relationship problems, fatigue, and workplace stress conspire against you to weaken your impulse control and lead you to seek comfort (often in ways that sabotage your goals) rather than pursuing change. Distress often yells while the need for change whispers.

Keep in mind that distress can be addressed. You can tackle stressful situations with a problem-solving orientation, and you can work to make things more manageable in your life. When you have achieved better management of your distress, you will be poised to resume the work of change again, and you can approach that work with renewed focus and vigor.

Achieve Greater Perspective

Another thing you can do when you feel bogged down by the disappointment of relapse is to broaden your perspective. Many times when we are upset by a difficult situation, we end up obsessing or stewing about it. Unfortunately, obsessive thoughts rarely go in a productive direction—they tend to spin around in your head and create anxiety instead of real solutions.

To get relief, you may need to take a step back and look at things from a different perspective. How can you achieve a bit of emotional distance from the problem? How can you shift your thinking so that you can recover from the physiological and psychological stress reaction that accompanies feelings of defeat?

One thing you may try is to see the humor in the situation. Is there an aspect of the situation that is genuinely funny? Is there a way to laugh at your human faults and shortcomings?

If it seems like your situation is no laughing matter, perhaps you can talk to someone (preferably an objective party whom you trust) about your relapse. Sharing your disappointment with someone else often helps you to widen your perspective.

Consider asking yourself: "How important will this situation be in one week? One month? One year? Five years?" Alternatively, find a way to be grateful that your situation is not worse than it is. Try to complete this statement: "I am certainly glad that I am not _____." (For example, "I am certainly glad that I am not living in my parents' basement." "I am certainly glad that I am not broke.")

A creative way to achieve greater perspective is to imagine yourself taking a helicopter ride or a hot air balloon ride above the difficult situation. Watch your problems beneath you on the ground getting smaller and smaller.

Consider the distressing thoughts that are spinning around in your head. Ask yourself:

- Are my thoughts based on fact?

- Are my thoughts protecting my life and health, or can I afford to get rid of them?

- Are my thoughts helping me to achieve my goals, or are they simply dragging me down?

- Will my thoughts help me to feel and act the way I need to feel and act to reach my money goals?

- Is my thinking in my best interest, or can I change it?

If you simply cannot achieve greater perspective on the problem, perhaps it would help to take a short break from your change efforts to shift toward an attitude of self-compassion.

Exercise Self-Compassion

There are times when we feel so deeply entrenched in a problem that we throw our hands up in the air and wave the white flag of surrender. Worse yet, we seek comfort from the very thing that got us into trouble in the first place. We blow our budget, we feel bad, and then we try to help ourselves feel better by spending more money. Researchers have cleverly named this the *what-the-hell effect*[3] (as in, "What the hell—I already blew it. Now I might as well really enjoy myself.")

The what-the-hell effect describes a cycle that starts with indulgence, moves on to feelings of regret (and guilt, shame, helplessness, and so forth), and consequently leads to even greater indulgence. As psychologist Kelly McGonigal describes it, "Giving in makes you feel bad about yourself, which motivates you to do something to feel better. And what's the cheapest, fastest strategy for feeling better? Often the very thing you feel bad about."[4]

Of course, this vicious cycle needs to be broken. Most people are aware of the need to interrupt this cycle. The way they try to fix the situation, however, is flawed. They try to employ guilt and self-criticism to regain a sense of control. "If I beat myself up enough for my mistake," they reason, "I can ensure that I will exercise greater self-control next time."

Unfortunately, guilt and self-criticism are associated with *diminished* motivation and self-control.[5] They are also two of the biggest predictors of depression, which leads to decreased energy, focus, and initiative. In many ways, guilt and self-criticism take you far away from the personal resources that you need to right the ship once it has begun to list.

Instead of guilt and self-criticism, you need tools that will actually enhance your motivation and self-control and give you a chance to correct your mistakes. *Self-compassion* and *self-forgiveness* are the proper tools for the job.

As soon as I mention self-compassion in the change group that I lead, my statement is inevitably met with resistance. Group members respond, "The last thing I need to do is be kinder to myself—that's the problem in the first place. I'm too lenient, and then I give myself permission to do the unhealthy things that I shouldn't do."

If this is your knee-jerk reaction to the idea of self-compassion, know that you are not alone. Many people believe that if they treat themselves with kindness, there will be no forces at work to correct mistakes or prevent them in the first place. But the reality is, self-compassion allows you to be open to learn from your experiences, your mistakes, and the feedback that you receive from other people. It does not sabotage accountability; it *increases* accountability.[6]

McGonigal explains it this way: If you perceive yourself as having failed and you cannot exercise forgiveness toward yourself, you end up with feelings of guilt, self-criticism, and self-hatred. Your priority, then, is to escape these uncomfortable feelings. You turn to unhealthy habits in an effort to comfort yourself.

Alternatively, if you perceive a setback as an opportunity to forgive yourself, you suffer far less pain, guilt, and self-criticism, if these feelings are even present at all. Because you do not have the need to escape uncomfortable feelings, you have mental energy available to figure out how the setback occurred and what to do differently next time. In this way, acting in a kind and compassionate way toward yourself increases flexible thinking and confidence in your personal resources.

David McArthur and Bruce McArthur make the point this way: *"Many people are afraid to forgive because they feel they must remember the wrong or they will not learn from it. The opposite is true. Through forgiveness, the wrong is released from its emotional stranglehold on us so that we can learn from it. Through the power and intelligence of the heart, the release of forgiveness brings expanded intelligence to work with the situation more effectively."*

Change flows naturally when you treat yourself with kindness while opening up to your mistakes. But if you are not accustomed to treating yourself with compassion, where do you begin? Author Christopher Germer describes several pathways to self-compassion.[7] One or more of these pathways may appeal to you.

First, there is a *physical* pathway to self-compassion. These are basic self-care strategies that prompt you to release the tension and stress that builds up in your body. Recall from the chapter on self-efficacy (chapter six) that you routinely check in with yourself to gather data about your physiological state (level of tension, arousal, energy, and so forth). You then interpret this data and use it to estimate how ready you feel to take on your goal. You feel more ready when you are not bothered by negative physical states. Activities that reduce physical tension and stress are basic tasks such as getting enough sleep, eating properly, getting enough exercise, and softening the breath.

Second, Germer writes about a *mental* pathway to self-compassion. You are kind to yourself mentally when you recognize that you are obsessing or ruminating about unhelpful thoughts and then work to create the conditions in which you let go of those thoughts. This could mean that you cultivate a mindfulness practice (as described in chapter eight). Or, it could mean that you train yourself to use a specific strategy for putting things in proper perspective (described earlier in this chapter).

Perhaps the most important pathway to self-compassion is the *emotional* one. When you are kind to yourself emotionally, you stop and befriend your painful emotions instead of fighting against them. When you make a money mistake, you take a moment to notice how you are feeling. Whatever comes up, you try to meet it with an attitude of curiosity, non-judgment, openness, and acceptance. "Oh, there are those feelings of guilt and self-criticism again—I recognize them. Let me see if I can sit with them quietly rather than rushing to escape from them."

After becoming acquainted with your emotions, imagine how you would treat a good friend if she made the same financial mistake. Humans are often much better at extending kindness and forgiveness to other people than sharing the same gifts with themselves. If you can imagine what you would say to a friend who has faltered financially, this helps you learn how to forgive yourself. What words of understanding and support would you offer to your friend who has experienced the same setback? How would you encourage her to return to her goal-directed efforts? Borrowing this outside perspective will give you hints about how to meet your own mistakes with grace and kindness.

Think through all of the ideas that were presented in this chapter. Many of them can be applied when obstacles arise in any life venture, not just in a financial change project. I hope you have gained an awareness of the variety of actions you can take even when you feel a complete lack of control and hope.

Having a regular troubleshooting strategy will allow you to maintain your new healthy habits over time with minimal disruption. It is the key to experiencing a successful *maintenance stage of change*, which is the topic of chapter fourteen.

Reflection Questions

Think of a time in the past when you were working on a healthy new money habit and you experienced a relapse. How did you know it was a relapse rather than a lapse? What was the most important lesson you learned from the relapse?

What is your favorite method of widening your perspective when you get caught in a narrow and negative way of looking at things?

How can you treat yourself with kindness and compassion the next time you experience a setback on the journey toward your financial goal?

Chapter Fourteen:
Maintenance

"Even if you're on the right track, you'll get run over if you just sit there."

-Will Rogers

"It wasn't raining when Noah built the ark."

-Howard Ruff

"Become a possibilitarian. No matter how dark things seem to be or actually are, raise your sights and see possibilities—always see them, for they're always there."

-Norman Vincent Peale

If you think back to the idea of the stages of change,[1] you will recall that when you are in the *action* stage (stage four), you are actively taking steps to change a money habit. Eventually, you want to make it to the *termination* stage (stage six), the stage in which the new habit feels more natural, automatic, and effortless. In stage six, you have complete confidence in your new, healthy behavior and feel certain that you will not return to your old, unhealthy habit.

To get from stage four to stage six, you have to pass through the *maintenance* stage. As the name suggests, the maintenance stage is about sticking to your change plan despite any circumstances that challenge your commitment and your confidence.

The main task that helps you with maintenance is called *relapse prevention*. During relapse prevention, you try to become aware of the situations or conditions that might tempt you to slip back into your old behavior patterns, and you plan how you will cope with these temptations. In other words, you think ahead during your good periods about how you might handle the more difficult times.

In this chapter, you will learn how to build an individualized relapse prevention plan. You will also take a step back to look at the larger picture of money in your life—how much value to place on money, and the ways in which money can support your overall well-being.

Relapse Prevention Plans

When challenging life situations come along, they may lead you to abandon your newly-acquired coping skills. Or, they may lead to an exacerbation of your original money troubles. That is why it is worthwhile to build a relapse prevention plan. Just as a stitch in time saves nine, a good relapse prevention plan can prevent a minor lapse from decompensating into a full-blown relapse.

Begin by thinking back over the book. What did you learn that was most meaningful to you? What worked for you, and what didn't work for you? What were your most successful behavioral experiments? How did your efforts lead to change? What strategies worked so well for you, they are sure to be a part of any of your future change efforts?

Now list the factors that may interfere with your efforts to continue with the change skills that you have learned. Think through all of the possible internal barriers, such as faulty memory, distraction, increased personal stress, or a diminished supply of self-control. Another common internal barrier is the discouraging observation that the financial outcomes you observe do not seem to correspond to the effort you have been putting into your change project. Perhaps you feel as though you have been working hard, but you do not have anything to show for it. You stop to take a look around and conclude, "It seems like it should be better/easier by now."

Once you have finished generating a list of internal barriers, think through the external barriers that may arise. External barriers may include time constraints, inconvenience, or a failure to be supported by the environment. As you learned in chapter ten, a lack of encouragement from the people around you can be a huge deterrent to your progress.

Next, list the high-risk situations that are coming up in your life that may undermine your ability to maintain your new, healthy money habit. Common high-risk situations include life transitions (think marriage, divorce, moving, changing jobs, or having a baby), social occasions, stressful events, and breaks from your normal life routine. When your routine changes abruptly, you lose the ability to rely on the action triggers and implementation intentions that you have established, and you are bombarded by a whole new set of temptations.

For each barrier and high-risk situation you have listed, consider how you can get yourself back on track.

Examples:

Potential Problem: *It is possible that at some point in the future, I will feel discouraged that my savings account is not growing as fast as I would like. If I feel like I am not making progress, I will be tempted to revert back to my former spending habits.*

Solution: *I will remind myself that self-disappointment and self-criticism lead to diminished motivation and greater indulgence. I will find a way to be patient with myself. Perhaps I will talk through my self-disappointment with a friend and then look at my net worth spreadsheet to appreciate the progress I have made.*

Potential Problem: *October is the most stressful month at my workplace. During that month, my anxiety and sleep deprivation increase while my supply of impulse control falls. I will likely be tempted to overspend to regulate my mood.*

Solution: *I will build extra (free) self-care activities into my schedule that month. I will invite my coworkers to join me and will pencil these activities into my calendar. If my coworkers choose not to join me, I will ask them to help me stay accountable to my healthy plans.*

The next step in building a relapse prevention plan is to create a "panic plan." With a predetermined panic plan, instead of panicking when your financial change efforts fail, you can refer to a detailed list of things that you have identified to be helpful in keeping up your motivation. Making the list ahead of time will give you the guidance to take action when things go off-course. The more specific you make the plan, the easier it will be to follow. Your list can include the resources, options, skills, and techniques that are available to you.

Example:

Panic Plan: *When I am panicking and feel hopeless about my ability to change my financial habits, I will take a break, ask my financial educator to help me pinpoint exactly what is going wrong, and then establish one simple rule, action trigger, or implementation intention that will help me get back on track.*

Now consider this: What will you do when you have a bad day and you cannot seem to get back on track, no matter what you do? This is a good time to be careful how you are thinking about, judging, or criticizing yourself and your efforts. Perhaps you can replace your self-critical statements with kindness and compassion toward the self. Perhaps you can remind yourself that everyone experiences setbacks. Or remind yourself that change is a winding road, and tomorrow will probably be better. Find a way to achieve a greater perspective and to recall the upward spiral of change.

What will I do when I have a bad day and cannot seem to get back on track with my financial change efforts?

What are the coping thoughts I will think when I have a bad day and cannot seem to get back on track?

You cannot anticipate all of the problematic circumstances that could possibly arise in the future. The goal is to develop the belief that you have the tools to respond appropriately to future challenges. Write an encouraging statement about your confidence in your ability to cope with problems.

How will I encourage myself when I need confidence in my ability to cope with challenges?

Minor setbacks are inevitable and do not signal total failure. Watch out for hopeless thinking or all-or-nothing thinking (for example,

"Well my finances are not responding to my change efforts, so I might as well give up trying.")

How will I remind myself that small setbacks do not mean total failure?

Finally, remember that social support can be one of your most powerful change tools. Make sure you share your change goal with the supportive people in your life, and ask for the specific assistance you need.

Who are the supportive people in my life to whom I can make myself accountable for further practice of my new skills?

Congratulations—you've done it! Not only have you started changing your money habits, but you've designed a plan to keep the change going well into the future.

The Happy Medium

Before the book draws to a close, there is one more issue to consider: What is the proper place to give to money in the grand scheme of your life? Throughout the book, you have been asked to focus intently on money. You have been encouraged to identify financial dreams and values that motivate you to take action. You have been taught a set of skills for monitoring your money habits and remaining mindful of the financial choices you make every day. Evidence shows that *making money a priority gives you the drive to succeed financially.*

At the same time, research suggests that hyper-consumerism and materialism can actually be toxic to your happiness.[2-3] If you place too much of your focus on wanting luxuries or valuing money more highly than relationships, this works against your overall sense of well-being.[3] One study of more than 7,000 college students from more than 41 countries showed a negative correlation between the extent to which the students placed value on money and their overall life satisfaction.[4] In other words, the more they placed an emphasis on money, the less satisfied they were with their lives.

Other studies have examined groups of people who lead lifestyles that de-emphasize material goods. One study compared Americans who led a "voluntarily simple" lifestyle (that is, a lifestyle marked by thrifty behaviors) to a matched sample of "mainstream" people.[5] This study showed that the voluntarily simple individuals enjoyed a subjective experience that was marked by a higher ratio of pleasant to unpleasant emotions.

A different study examined the overall well-being of a group of Amish people living in the Midwestern region of the United States.[6] These individuals, as a matter of religious principle, choose to lead a materially-simple lifestyle without many of the modern conveniences and technologies that are commonplace elsewhere today. The researchers found that on average, the members of this group reported levels of positive emotions and life satisfaction that were substantially above neutral.

A common explanation for these findings is that if you focus less on the quest for money in your life, it allows more space for contentment and less opportunity for a sense of failed aspirations.[7] Another explanation is that if you do not have to expend your personal resources on building your finances, you can focus more on tending to your relationships—and relationships have been shown to be crucial to personal happiness.[8]

In the grand scheme of things, then, you are striving for a "happy medium" in which you value your financial dreams enough to keep going in a healthy direction, but your desire for money does not distract you from the blessings of life that are truly lasting and meaningful. It is a tricky balance that is endlessly shifting.

Money and Well-Being

The relationship between money and happiness is complex. Poverty takes a psychological toll on people and their overall sense of well-being. But having enough money does not guarantee happiness. Increases in wealth generally lead to increases in life satisfaction. But we adapt to increases in wealth over time, and they play a smaller and smaller role in making us happy.

In general, people are happy when their income increases because money offers more psychological security, more choices, and the ability to pursue meaningful goals.[7] Research suggests that to stretch the value of your money even further, you should spend your money on experiences rather than material purchases.[9]

Invest in new experiences that you can share with the people in your life. The memories of these experiences will remain positive (and even get better!) over time. "While individuals may adapt to new physical consumer goods they are more likely to revise memories of experiences to make them more positive."[10] Plus, experiences offer you the chance to engage in rewarding social interaction and thereby strengthen your relationships. As you learned earlier, social connection is believed to be the key to personal fulfillment.

Section Summary

In this section, you have learned how to carry your new habits into the future, and you have gathered ideas for overcoming the obstacles that may arise.

My wish for you, as you come to the end of this book, is financial health: both the skills to reach your money goals, and the wisdom to know the proper place of money in your life. Beyond that, I wish you confidence for changing your life, one habit at a time. Through your change journey, may you come to know your strength and resiliency, and may you surprise yourself with what is possible.

Notes

Understanding the Problem

1. Low, A. (1965). *What's in Mommy's pocketbook?* New York: Golden Press.

2. Wiseman, R. (2009). *59 Seconds: Think a little change a lot.* New York: Alfred A. Knopf.

3. Employee Benefit Research Institute, American Savings Education Council, & Mathew Greenwald and Associates (2009). *Retirement Confidence Survey.*

4. Sethi, A., Mischel, W., Aber, L., Shoda, Y., & Rodriguez, M. (2000). The role of strategic attention deployment in development of self-regulation: Predicting preschoolers' delay of gratification from mother-toddler interactions. *Developmental Psychology, 36,* 767-777.

5. Gailliot, M. T., Mead, N. L., & Baumeister, R. F. (2008). Self-regulation. In O. P. John, R. W., Robbins, & L. A. Pervin (Eds.), *Handbook of personality: Theory and research* (pp. 472-491). New York: The Guilford Press.

6. Brehm, J. W. (1966). *A theory of psychological reactance.* Academic Press.

7. Brehm, S. S., & Brehm, J. W. (1981). *Psychological reactance: A theory of freedom and control.* Academic Press.

8. Belsky, G., & Gilovich, T. (1999). *Why smart people make big money mistakes and how to correct them: Lessons from the new science of behavioral economics.* New York: Simon & Schuster.

9,10. Ben-Shahar, T. (2009). *The pursuit of perfect: How to stop chasing perfection and start living a richer, happier life.* New York: McGraw Hill.

11. Norcross, J. C., Ratzin, A. C., & Payne, D. (1989). Ringing in the New Year: The change process and reported outcomes of resolutions. *Addictive Behaviors, 14,* 205-212.

12. Haidt, J. (2006). *The happiness hypothesis: Finding modern truth in ancient wisdom*. New York: Basic Books.

13. Dweck, C. (2006). *Mindset: The new psychology of success*. New York: Ballantine Books.

14. Prochaska, J. O., Norcross, J. C., & DiClemente, C. C. (1994). *Changing for good: A revolutionary six-stage program for overcoming bad habits and moving your life positively forward*. New York: HarperCollins.

Preparing for Change

1. Ericsson, K. A., Krampe, R. T., & Tesch-Roemer, C. (1993). The role of deliberate practice in the acquisition of expert performance. *Psychological Review, 100*, 363-406.

2. Wing, R. R., & Hill, J. O. (2001). Successful weight loss maintenance. *Annual Review of Nutrition, 21*, 323-341.

3. Houser-Marko, L., & Sheldon, K. M. (2006). Motivating behavioral persistence: The self-as-doer construct. *Personality and Social Psychology Bulletin, 32*, 1037-1049.

4. Hollenbeck, J., Williams, C., & Klein, H. (1989). An empirical examination of the antecedents of commitment to difficult goals. *Journal of Applied Psychology, 74*, 18-23.

5. Lewis, T. Amini, F., & Lannon, R. (2000). *A general theory of love*. New York: Random House.

6. Heath, C., & Heath, D. (2010). *Switch: How to change things when change is hard*. New York: Broadway Books.

7. Dweck, C. (2006). *Mindset: The new psychology of success*. New York: Ballantine Books.

Establishing Goals and Intentions

1. Heath, C., & Heath, D. (2010). *Switch: How to change things when change is hard*. New York: Broadway Books.

2. Ben-Shahar, T. (2009). *The pursuit of perfect: How to stop chasing perfection and start living a richer, happier life.* New York: McGraw Hill.

3. Locke, E. A., & Latham, G. P. (2002). Building a practically useful theory of goal setting and task motivation: A 35-year odyssey. *American Psychologist, 57,* 705-717.

4. Wiseman, R. (2009). *59 Seconds: Think a little, change a lot.* New York: Alfred A. Knopf.

5. Cialdini, R. & Goldstein, N. (2004). Social influence: Compliance and conformity. *Annual Review of Psychology, 55,* 591-621.

6. Davidson, R., University of Wisconsin, statement to the Dalai Lama at the 2004 Mind Conference, quoted in *Train Your Mind, Change Your Brain* (Begley, S., 2007, New York: Ballantine Books).

7. Eker, T. H. (2005). *Secrets of the millionaire mind: Mastering the inner game of wealth.* New York: Collins.

8. Carver, C. S., & Scheier, M. F. (1981). *Attention and self-regulation: A control-theory approach to human behavior.* New York: Springer.

9. Seligman, M. E. P. (2002). *Authentic happiness: Using the new positive psychology to realize your potential for lasting fulfillment.* New York: Simon & Schuster.

10. Ferriss, T. (2007). *The 4-hour workweek: Escape 9-5, live anywhere, and join the new rich.* New York: Crown Publishers.

11. Locke, E. A. (1996). Motivation through conscious goal setting. *Applied and Preventive Psychology, 5,* 117-124.

12. Patterson, K., Grenny, J., Maxfield, D., McMillan, R., & Switzler, A. (2011). *Change anything: The new science of personal success.* New York: Hachette Book Group.

13. Gollwitzer, P. M., & Sheeran, P. (2006). Implementation intentions and goal achievement: A meta-analysis of effects and processes. *Advances in Experimental Social Psychology, 38,* 69-119.

Self-Monitoring

1. Korotitsch, W. J., & Nelson-Gray, R. O. (1999). An overview of self-monitoring research in assessment and treatment. *Psychological Assessment, 11*, 415-425.

2. Ornstein, R. E., & Sobel, D. (1990). *Healthy pleasures.* Cambridge, MA: Da Capo Press.

3. Rozensky, R. H. (1974). The effect of timing of self-monitoring behavior on reducing cigarette consumption. *Journal of Behavior Therapy and Experimental Psychiatry, 5*, 301-303.

4. Bellack, A. S., Rozensky, R., & Schwartz, J. (1974). A comparison of two forms of self-monitoring in a behavioral weight reduction program. *Behavior Therapy, 5*, 523-530.

5. Shapiro, A. (2008, July 3). Why we spend more using credit versus cash [Radio broadcast episode]. In E. McDonnell (Producer) *Morning Edition.* Washington, D.C.: National Public Radio.

Stages of Change

1. Prochaska, J. O., DiClemente, C. C., & Norcross, J. C. (1992). In search of how people change: Applications to addictive behaviors. *American Psychologist, 47,* 1102-1114.

2. Prochaska, J. O., Norcross, J., & DiClemente, C. (1995). *Changing for good: A revolutionary six-stage program for overcoming bad habits and moving your life positively forward.* New York: HarperCollins.

3. Svenson, O. (1981). Are we all less risky and more skillful than our fellow drivers? *Acta Psychologica, 47*, 143-148.

Self-Efficacy

1. Canning, I., Sherman, E., Unwin, G. (Producers), & Hooper, T. (Director). (2011). *The king's speech* [Motion picture]. United Kingdom: Momentum Pictures.

2. Bandura, A. (1977). Self-efficacy: Toward a unifying theory of behavioral change. *Psychological Review, 84*, 191-215.

3. Bandura, A. (1997). *Self-efficacy: The exercise of control.* New York: W. H. Freeman and Company.

4. Bandura, A. (1986). *Social foundations of thought and action: A social cognitive theory* (p. 395). Englewood Cliffs, NJ: Prentice Hall.

5. Heath, C., & Heath, D. (2010). *Switch: How to change things when change is hard.* New York: Broadway Books.

6. Weick, K. E. (1984). Small wins: Redefining the scale of social problems. *American Psychologist, 39*, 40-49.

Persistence

1. Duckworth, A. L, Peterson, C., Matthews, M. D., & Kelly, D. R. (2007). Grit: Perseverance and passion for long-term goals. *Journal of Personality and Social Psychology, 92*, 1087-1101.

2. Ryan, R. M., & Deci, E. L. (2000). Self-determination theory and the facilitation of intrinsic motivation, social development, and well-being. *American Psychologist, 55*, 68-78.

3. Patterson, K., Grenny, J., Maxfield, D., McMillan, R., & Switzler, A. (2011). *Change anything: The new science of personal success.* New York: Hachette Book Group.

4. Masten, A. S., & Reed, M. J. (2002). Resilience in development. In C. R. Snyder & S. J. Lopez (Eds.), *Handbook of Positive Psychology* (pp. 74-88). New York: Oxford University Press.

5. Bonanno, G. A. (2004). Loss, trauma, and human resilience: Have we underestimated the capacity to thrive after extremely aversive events? *American Psychologist, 59*, 20-28.

6. Cowen, E. L., & Work, W. C. (1988). Resilient children, psychological wellness, and primary prevention. *American Journal of Community Psychology, 16*, 591-607.

7. Elliott, T. R., Kurylo, M., & Rivera, P. (2002). Positive growth following acquired physical disability. In C. R. Snyder & S. J. Lopez (Eds.), *Handbook of Positive Psychology* (pp. 687-699). New York: Oxford University Press.

8. Tugade, M. M., & Fredrickson, B. L. (2004). Resilient individuals use positive emotions to bounce back from negative emotional experiences. *Journal of Personality and Social Psychology, 86*, 320-333.

9. Lemov, D., Woolway, E., & Yezzi, K. (2012). *Practice perfect: 42 rules for getting better at getting better*. San Francisco: Jossey-Bass.

Impulse Control

1. Kestner, J., Leithinger, D., Jung, J., & Petersen, M. (2009). Proverbial wallet: Tangible interface for financial awareness. Proceedings of the 3rd International Conference on Tangible and Embedded Interaction.

2. Hung, I. W., & Labroo, A. A. (2011). From firm muscles to firm willpower: Understanding the role of embodied cognition in self-regulation. *Journal of Consumer Research, 37*, 1046-1064.

3. Mischel, W., Ebbesen, E. B., & Zeiss, A. R. (1972). Cognitive and attentional mechanisms in delay of gratification. *Journal of Personality and Social Psychology, 21*, 204-221.

4. Shoda, Y., Mischel, W., & Peake, P. (1990). Predicting adolescent cognitive and self-regulatory competencies from preschool delay of gratification: Identifying diagnostic conditions. *Developmental Psychology, 6*, 978-986.

5. Moffitt, T. E., et al. (2011). A gradient of childhood self-control predicts health, wealth, and public safety. Proceedings of the National Academy of Sciences, 108, 2963-2968.

6. Baumeister, R. F., Bratslavsky, E., Muraven, M., & Tice, D. M. (1998). Ego-depletion: Is the active self a limited resource? *Journal of Personality and Social Psychology, 74*, 1252-1265.

7. Muraven, M., Tice, D. M., & Baumeister, R. F. (1998). Self-control as a limited resource: Regulatory depletion patterns. *Journal of Personality and Social Psychology, 74*, 774-789.

8. Vohs, K. D., Baumeister, R. F., Schmeichel, B. J., Twenge, J. M., Nelson, N. M., & Tice, D. M. (2008). Making choices impairs subsequent self-control: A limited-resource account of decision making, self-regulation, and active initiative. *Journal of Personality and Social Psychology, 94*, 883-898.

9. Grandey, A. A. (2000). Emotional regulation in the workplace: A new way to conceptualize emotional labor. *Journal of Occupational Health Psychology, 5*, 95-110.

10. Wegner, D. M.., Schneider, D. J., Carter, S. R., & White, T. L. (1987). Paradoxical effects of thought suppression. *Journal of Personality and Social Psychology, 53*, 5-13.

11. Wegner, D. M. (1994). Ironic processes of mental control. *Psychological Review, 101*, 34-52.

12. Giuliano, R. J., & Wicha, N. Y. Y. (2010). Why the white bear is still there: Electrophysiological evidence for ironic semantic activation during thought suppression. *Brain Research, 1316*, 62-74.

13. Tice, D. M., Bratslavsky, E., & Baumeister, R. F. (2001). Emotional distress regulation takes precedence over impulse control: If you feel bad, do it! *Journal of Personality and Social Psychology, 80*, 53-67.

14. Lehrer, J. (2009). Blame it on the brain. *Wall Street Journal*, December 26, 2009.

15. McCaul, K. D., & Malott, J. M. (1984). Distraction and coping with pain. *Psychological Bulletin, 95*, 516-533.

16. Harris, R. (2009). *ACT made simple: An easy-to-read primer on acceptance and commitment therapy*. Oakland, CA: New Harbinger.

17. Forman, E. M., Hoffman, K. L., McGrath, K. B., Herbert, J. D., Brandsma, L. L., & Lowe, M. R. (2007). A comparison of acceptance- and control-based strategies for coping with food cravings: An analog study. *Behaviour Research and Therapy, 45*, 2372-86.

18. Duckworth, A. L., & Seligman, M. E. P. (2005). Self-discipline outdoes IQ in predicting academic performance of adolescents. *Psychological Science, 16*, 939-944.

19. Cameron, C. E., McClelland, M. M., Connor, C. M., Jewkes, A. M., Farris, C. L., & Morrison, F. J. (2008). Touch your toes! Developing a direct measure of behavioral regulation in early childhood. *Early Childhood Research Quarterly, 23*, 141-158.

20. Tominey, S., & McClelland, M. M. (2008, April). "And when they woke up, they were monkeys! Using class room games to promote preschoolers' self-regulation and school readiness. Poster presented at the biennial Conference on Human Development, Indianapolis, IN.

21. Duckworth, A. L., Peterson, C., Matthews, M. D., & Kelly, D. R. (2007). Grit: Perseverance and passion for long-term goals. *Journal of Personality and Social Psychology, 92*, 1087-1101.

22. McGonigal, K. (2012). *The willpower instinct: How self-control works, why it matters, and what you can do to get more of it*. New York: Avery.

23. Oaten, M., & Cheng, K. (2007). Improvements in self-control from financial monitoring. *Journal of Economic Psychology, 28*, 487-501.

24. Segerstrom, S. C., Hardy, J. K., Evans, D. R., & Winters, N. F. (2012). Pause and plan: Self-regulation and the heart. In R. A. Wright (Ed.), *How motivation affects cardiovascular response: Mechanisms and applications* (pp. 181-198). Washington, DC: American Psychological Association.

25. Song, H. S., & Lehrer, P. M. (2003). The effects of specific respiratory rates on heart rate and heart rate variability. *Applied Psychophysiology and Biofeedback, 28*, 13-23.

Using the Environment in Your Favor

1. For example, see the studies summarized in Dean, J. (2013). *Making habits, breaking habits: Why we do things, why we don't, and how to make any change stick*. Great Britain: Oneworld Publications.

2. Heath, C., & Heath, D. (2010). *Switch: How to change things when change is hard*. New York: Broadway Books.

3. Samuelson, W., & Zeckhauser, R. (1988). Status quo bias in decision making. *Journal of Risk and Uncertainty, 1*, 7-59.

4. Thaler, R. H., & Sunstein, C. R. (2009). *Nudge: Improving decisions about health, wealth, and happiness*. New York: Penguin.

Change in a Social Context

1. Patterson, K., Grenny, J., Maxfield, D., McMillan, R., & Switzler, A. (2011). *Change anything: The new science of personal success*. New York: Hachette Book Group.

2. Heatherley, J. L. (2004). *Balcony people (revised edition)*. Georgetown, TX: Balcony Publishing, Inc.

Taming Self-Sabotaging Thoughts

1. Beck, A. T., Rush, A. J., Shaw, B. F., & Emery, G. (1979). *Cognitive therapy of depression*. New York: Guilford.

2. Berdik, C. (2012). *Mind over mind: The surprising power of expectations*. New York: Current.

Harnessing the Power of Emotion

1. Haidt, J. (2006). *The happiness hypothesis: Finding modern truth in ancient wisdom*. New York: Basic Books.

2. Wansink, B. (2007). *Mindless eating: Why we eat more than we think*. New York: Random House.

3. Loewenstein, G. (1996). Out of control: Visceral influences on behavior. *Organizational Behavior and Human Decision Processes, 65,* 272-292.

4. Heath, C., & Heath, D. (2010). *Switch: How to change things when change is hard.* New York: Broadway Books.

5. Thaler, R. H., & Sunstein, C. R. (2008). *Nudge: Improving decisions about health, wealth, and happiness.* New York: Penguin.

6. Linehan, M. M. (1993). *Skills training manual for treating borderline personality disorder.* New York: Guilford Press.

7. Linehan, M. M. (1993). *Cognitive-behavioral treatment of borderline personality disorder.* New York: Guilford Press.

8. Csikszentmihalyi, M. (1990). *Flow: The psychology of optimal experience.* New York: Harper Collins.

9. Wilson, T. D., & Gilbert, D. T. (2003). Affective forecasting. In M. P. Zanna (Ed.), *Advances in Experimental Social Psychology* (Vol. 35, pp. 345-411). Amsterdam: Academic Press.

10. Dunn, E. W., Aknin, L., & Norton, M. I. (2008). Spending money on others promotes happiness. *Science, 319,* 1687-1688.

11. Ruby, M. B., Dunn, E. W., Perrino, A., Gillis, R., & Viel, S. (2011). The invisible benefits of exercise. *Health Psychology, 30,* 67-74.

Troubleshooting

1. Dweck, C. (2006). *Mindset: The new psychology of success.* New York: Ballantine Books.

2. Prochaska, J. O., Norcross, J., & DiClemente, C. (1995). *Changing for good: A revolutionary six-stage program for overcoming bad habits and moving your life positively forward.* New York: HarperCollins.

3. Polivy, J., & Herman, C. P. (1985). Dieting and binging: A causal analysis. *American Psychologist, 40,* 193-201.

4. McGonigal, K. (2012). *The willpower instinct: How self-control works, why it matters, and what you can do to get more of it*. New York: Avery.

5. Kelly McGonigal does an excellent review of these studies in her book, *The willpower instinct*.

6. Neff, K. D., Kirkpatrick, K. L., & Rude, S. S. (2007). Self-compassion and adaptive psychological functioning. *Journal of Research in Personality, 41*, 139-154.

7. Germer, C. K. (2009). *The mindful path to self-compassion: Freeing yourself from destructive thoughts and emotions*. New York: Guilford.

Maintenance

1. Prochaska, J. O., DiClemente, C. C., & Norcross, J. C. (1992). In search of how people change: Applications to addictive behaviors. *American Psychologist, 47*, 1102-1114.

2. Kasser, T. (2003). *The high price of materialism*. Cambridge, MA: MIT Press.

3. Kasser, T., & Ryan, R. M. (1993). A dark side of the American dream: Correlates of financial success as a central life aspiration. *Journal of Personality and Social Psychology, 65*, 410-422.

4. Diener, E., & Oishi, S. (2000). Money and happiness: Income and subjective well-being across nations. In E. Diener & E. M. Suh (Eds.), *Culture and subjective well-being* (pp. 185-218). Cambridge, MA: MIT Press.

5. Brown, K. W., & Kasser, T. (2005). Are psychological and ecological well-being compatible? The role of values, mindfulness, and lifestyle. *Social Indicators Research, 74*, 349-368.

6. Biswas-Diener, R. Vitterso, J., & Diener, E. (2005). Most people are pretty happy, but there is cultural variation: The Inughuit, the Amish, and the Maasai. *Journal of Happiness Studies, 6*, 205-226.

7. Diener, E., & Biswas-Diener, R. (2008). *Happiness: Unlocking the mysteries of psychological wealth*. Boston, MA: Blackwell.

8. Diener, E., & Seligman, M. E. P. (2002). Very happy people. *Psychological Science, 13*, 80-83.

9. Van Boven, L., & Gilovich, T. (2003). To do or to have? That is the question. *Journal of Personality and Social Psychology, 85*, 1193-1202.

10. Mitchell, T. R., Thompson, L., Peterson, E., & Cronk, R. (1997). Temporal adjustments in the evaluation of events: The "rosy view." *Journal of Experimental Social Psychology, 33*, 421-448.